T0214502

Lecture Notes in Computer Science 11732

More information about this series at http://www.springer.com/series/7408

Radu Calinescu · Felicita Di Giandomenico (Eds.)

Software Engineering for Resilient Systems

11th International Workshop, SERENE 2019
Naples, Italy, September 17, 2019
Proceedings

Editors
Radu Calinescu (iD)
University of York
York, UK

Felicita Di Giandomenico (iD)
ISTI-CNR
Pisa, Italy

ISSN 0302-9743   ISSN 1611-3349 (electronic)
Lecture Notes in Computer Science
ISBN 978-3-030-30855-1   ISBN 978-3-030-30856-8 (eBook)
https://doi.org/10.1007/978-3-030-30856-8

LNCS Sublibrary: SL2 – Programming and Software Engineering

This Springer imprint is published by the registered company Springer Nature Switzerland AG
The registered company address is: Gewerbestrasse 11, 6330 Cham, Switzerland

Preface

This volume contains the proceedings of the 11th International Workshop on Software Engineering for Resilient Systems (SERENE 2019). SERENE 2019 took place in Naples, Italy, on September 17, 2019. The SERENE workshop is an annual event that brings together leading researchers and practitioners from academia and industry, to advance the state of the art and to identify open challenges in the software engineering of resilient systems.

The 2019 edition of SERENE provided a forum for the exchange of ideas on advances in areas of software engineering for resilient systems, including, but not limited to:

Development of resilient systems

- Engineering processes for resilient systems
- Requirements engineering and re-engineering for resilience
- Frameworks, patterns, and software architectures for resilience
- Engineering of self-healing autonomic systems
- Design of trustworthy and intrusion-safe systems
- Resilience at run-time (mechanisms, reasoning, and adaptation)
- Resilience and dependability (resilience vs. robustness, dependable vs. adaptive systems)

Verification, validation and evaluation of resilience

- Modeling and model based analysis of resilience properties
- Formal and semi-formal techniques for verification and validation
- Experimental evaluations of resilient systems
- Quantitative approaches to ensuring resilience
- Resilience prediction

Case studies and applications

- Empirical studies in the domain of resilient systems
- Methodologies adopted in industrial contexts
- Cloud computing and resilient service provisioning
- Resilience for data-driven systems (e.g., big data-based adaption and resilience)
- Resilient cyber-physical systems and infrastructures
- Global aspects of resilience engineering: education, training, and cooperation

SERENE 2019 attracted 12 submissions, from which 5 submissions were accepted as full papers and 4 submissions were accepted as short papers. Every submission received at least three rigorous reviews. We would like to express our gratitude to the Program Committee members and the additional reviewers, who actively participated in reviewing and discussing the submissions.

In addition to the high-quality papers selected by the Program Committee, SERENE 2019 featured an enlightening keynote and an invited paper. The keynote addressed the ethics and privacy of autonomous systems and was presented by Paola Inverardi, professor at the University of L'Aquila, the recipient of the 2013 IEEE TCSE Distinguished Service Award, and a leading expert in software engineering. The invited paper, contributed by Jesper Andersson, Vincenzo Grassi, Raffaela Mirandola, and Diego Perez-Palacin, introduced a unifying conceptual framework for the characterization of system resilience.

Since 2015 SERENE has become part of a major European dependability forum – the European Dependable Computing Conference (EDCC). We would like to thank the Organizing Committee of EDCC 2019 for their help in organizing the workshop. We are also grateful to EasyChair for facilitating the SERENE 2019 submission, reviewing, and proceedings generation.

September 2019   Radu Calinescu
                                                          Felicita Di Giandomenico

Organization

Steering Committee

Didier Buchs	University of Geneva, Switzerland
Henry Muccini	University of L'Aquila, Italy
Patrizio Pelliccione	Chalmers University of Technology, Sweden
Alexander Romanovsky	Newcastle University, UK
Elena Troubitsyna	Royal Institute of Technology, Finland

Program Committee

Nuno Antunes	University of Coimbra, Portugal
Luciana Arantes	Universite Pierre et Marie Curie-Paris 6, France
Rami Bahsoon	University of Birmingham, UK
Silvia Bonomi	Sapienza University of Rome, Italy
Marsha Chechik	University of Toronto, Canada
Catello Di Martino	Bell Labs Alcatel-Lucent, USA
Giovanna Di Marzo Serugendo	University of Geneva, Switzerland
Lars Grunske	Humboldt University Berlin, Germany
Jérémie Guiochet	LAAS-CNRS, France
Dubravka Ilic	Space Systems Finland, Finland
Rolf Johansson	Autonomous Intelligent Driving, Sweden
Linas Laibinis	Åbo Akademi University, Finland
Raffaela Mirandola	Politecnico di Milano, Italy
Henry Muccini	University of L'Aquila, Italy
Roberto Natella	University of Naples Federico II, Italy
Patrizio Pelliccione	Chalmers University of Technology, Sweden
Genaina Rodrigues	University of Brasilia, Brazil
Francesca Saglietti	University of Erlangen-Nuremberg, Germany
Cristina Seceleanu	Mälardalen University, Sweden
Alin Stefanescu	University of Bucharest, Romania
Elena Troubitsyna	Royal Institute of Technology, Finland

Additional Reviewers

Eduard Paul Enoiu	Mälardalen University, Sweden
Rong Gu	Mälardalen University, Sweden

Contents

Security, Trust and Privacy Management

Keynote Paper

Ethics and Privacy in Autonomous Systems: A Software Exoskeleton to Empower the User

Paola Inverardi[✉]

Department of Information Engineering Computer Science
and Mathematics, University of L'Aquila, L'Aquila, Italy
paola.inverardi@univaq.it

Abstract. Software systems are increasingly autonomous in making decisions on behalf of potential users. In these systems, the power of self goes beyond the ability of substituting human agents operating on software systems and exceeds the system boundaries invading the user prerogatives. Privacy and ethical issues are at the top of the research agenda in (big) data management and AI, that offer a wide range of techniques often used as key (black-box) components of autonomous systems. In this extended abstract, I discuss these issues from the software system developer perspective that uses such black-box components and outline a new approach based on a partially synthesized software exoskeleton that empowers the user by mediating her interactions in order to preserve her privacy and ethical preferences.

Keywords: Ethics · Privacy · Software exoskeleton

1 The Digital Society

In our current world, citizens continuously interact with software systems, e.g., by using a mobile device or from on board of a (autonomous) car. This will happen more and more in the future, while we embed digitalizations in the fabric of society thus impacting the social, economic, and political spheres.

The digital world, denoted with the powerful metaphor of the mangrove societies by Floridi [8] will be increasingly dominated by autonomous systems that make decisions over and above the users or on behalf of them. Automatizing larger and larger portions of services and functionalities of the society inevitably impacts on user prerogatives and puts at danger the ethical and privacy sphere of citizens. Besides the known risks represented by, e.g., unauthorized disclosure and mining of personal data or access to restricted resources, and that are receiving a huge amount of attention there is a less evident but even more serious risk that is at the core of the fundamental rights of human being [9].

Supported by the University of L'Aquila - Italy.

R. Calinescu and F. Di Giandomenico (Eds.): SERENE 2019, LNCS 11732, pp. 3–8, 2019.
https://doi.org/10.1007/978-3-030-30856-8_1

Indeed, autonomous machine may tend to restrict the free space in a democratic society in which a human being can exercise her freedom of choice. That is the space of decisions that are left to any individuals when such decisions do not break fundamental rights and laws but are the expression of personal ethic. There is therefore the risk of massification and loss of individualities in a digital society where individuals are unpaired with respect to machines beyond the basic choice of accepting or not accepting the interaction with a machine with all the consequences this might imply. From the case of privacy preferences in the app domain [11] to the more complex case of autonomous driving cars [7] the potential user is left unprotected and inadequate in her interaction with the digital world.

The goal of the talk is to motivate and introduce the project EXOSOUL [5] that aims at equipping humans with an automatically generated exoskeleton, a software shield that protects them and their personal data via the mediation of all interactions with the digital world that would result in unacceptable or morally wrong behaviors according to their ethical and privacy preferences.

2   The Exosoul Vision and Challenges

The goal of EXOSOUL is to empower the users with a personalized exoskeleton that permits to control and mediate interactions according to the ethic profile of user. In the EXOSOUL approach privacy is considered, as it is in the philosophical setting, a dimension of ethics. Therefore, the exoskeleton is aware of the ethical preferences of the user and can interact accordingly with the surrounding systems.

The exoskeleton can take a whole spectrum of forms: from customized soft-libraries that the individual may deploy on the devices and systems being used, to a sophisticated software interface that an individual may *wear*, eventually deployed on a body chip. Exoskeletons development may also open business opportunities in the same way open source software did, which promoted the ethical principles of free software against the monopoly proprietary software producers. Indeed, building systems that embody ethical principles by design may also permit acquiring a competitive advantage in the market, as predicted in the recent Gartner Top 10 Strategic Technology Trends for 2019 [1]. Furthermore, bringing back to the user part of the (digital) control helps to solve liability issues in autonomous systems by readdressing responsibility to users according to their specified ethics.

The automatic realization of an individual exoskeleton starting from the ethics and privacy preferences of the user requires several challenges to face. In the ethical sphere, this requires to: (i) identify a space of ethics and privacy preferences for users, that we recognize in the concept of *soft ethics* [8], to assess their compatibility with regulations, and to orchestrate interactions of users endorsing different preferences, so as to prevent deadlocks and to promote best ethical practices in digital societies; (ii) infer ethics and privacy preferences from the user, given that neither a person nor a society apply moral categories separately, rather everyday morality is in constant flux among norms, utilitarian assessment of consequences, and evaluation of virtues.

The exoskeleton deals with two classes of interactions (see Fig. 1). The first one concerns interactions that involve the exchange of personal data, and as such impact the privacy dimension, notably interactions with mobile apps through mobile devices. The approach in EXOSOUL is to consider user data *active*, that is provided with mechanisms that govern their creation, destruction, use, and sharing according to the owner ethical preferences. Destruction is the basic means to provide the right to be forgotten, which requires to equip data with an apoptosis mechanism synthesized from the user's ethical and privacy preferences and whose enactment depends on the use the digital world makes of the data. The second one concerns the interaction with systems that have some degree of autonomy and that a user may want to ethically control. Autonomous vehicles and the so-called trolley problem represent a well-known case as exemplified in [7]. As part of the exoskeleton, there will be an *ethical actuator* synthesized out of the user's ethical preferences able to intercept the interactions between the autonomous engine and the machine actuators and to prevent behaviors that are not admissible by the ethical preferences.

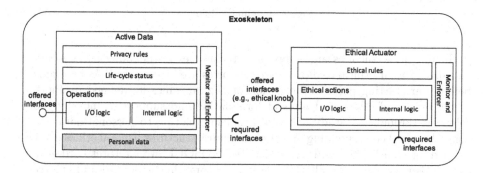

Fig. 1. The structure of the exoskeleton

This approach can be possible if the systems that wants to interact with an exoskeleton provided user, accept to disclose part of its interface. Although this requirement might be considered strong, it is indeed very current practice in system's interoperability once we lift the system *individual plus exoskeleton* at the systems interacting level. This means that together with the personalized shield also the architecture and protocol requirements the systems producers need to comply with are produced. EXOSOUL citizens will interact only with the part of the digital world that accepts their requirements. This introduces more symmetry in the producer/user roles and breaks the monopoly of producers.

3   The EXOSOUL Methodology

In this section, the methodology to obtain the exoskeletons is sketched (see Fig. 2).

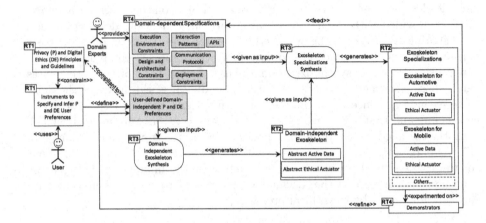

Fig. 2. The methodology

In RT1 logic theories and supporting techniques for enabling users to infer and specify their ethical and privacy preferences are investigated. As mentioned before, our starting point is the notion of Digital ethics [8] defined by Floridi as the branch of ethics that aims at formulating and supporting morally good solutions through the study of moral problems relating to personal data, (AI) algorithms and corresponding practices and infrastructures. Digital ethics can be divided into hard ethics and soft ethics. In EXOSOUL, we interpret hard ethics as the (democratic) societal ethics, that is the one that is defined and enforced by digital legislation. However, legislation does not cover everything, nor should it. The inhabitants of the digital world, e.g., companies and citizens, assess their role in the digital world by following their personal ethics, the soft ethics which deals with all the (moral) decisions that can be taken without trying to by-pass or change the hard ethics i.e. the existing regulation. Soft ethics is exactly what EXOSOUL aims to support in the personal exoskeleton while we expect hard ethics to be implemented by the systems/machine producers.

In Fig. 2, 'Privacy (P) and Digital Ethics (DE) Principles and Guidelines' refer to hard privacy and hard ethics that are defined and enforced by digital legislation. Instead, 'Instruments to Specify and Infer P and DE User Preferences' enable the user to define her soft privacy and soft ethics. The 'User-defined Domain independent P and DE Preferences' will be defined via a top-down approach (≪define≫ arrow), then refined and tuned up via a bottom-up approach (≪refine≫ arrow from 'Demonstrators'). RT2 conceptually defines the exoskeleton together with the techniques for manipulating it. RT3 investigates innovative synthesis techniques to generate exoskeletons so to reflect user privacy and ethical preferences. In the figure, artifacts provided by the users and domain experts are in light-gray. More precisely, user-defined domain-independent P and DE preferences are inferred and specified by end users of EXOSOUL through the instruments produced by RT1. In turn, this artifact is the input of the domain-independent exoskeleton synthesis. The other artifacts that are highlighted in light gray (see the Domain-dependent Specifications box) are provided by domain experts and contain the domain-dependent specifications that are given as input to the exoskeleton specializations synthesis in order to produce exoskeletons specialized for the accounted domains, e.g., mobile and automotive. These specifications will be provided by following the practical guidelines that will be established while developing the project demonstrators in RT4. The demonstrators will be used to assess the research and innovation outcomes of EXOSOUL.

The overall approach of EXOSOUL is defined at the architectural level. Indeed, the exoskeletons operate at the systems interaction levels, therefore synthesis techniques take the move from the research and practical experience matured by our group of research over the last decade [2–4,6,10,12,13].

4   Conclusions

In this extended abstract, I have shortly described the EXOSOUL project. EXOSOUL addresses a problem of utmost concern nowadays: the impact that autonomous technologies have and will have on the ethical sphere of individuals in the digital societies. EXOSOUL takes a specific and original approach that is to protect and empower the citizen. Differently to most of the approches at present advocated based on developers responsability, accountability and transparency see for example the Ethics Guidelines for Trustworthy AI produced by the High-Level Expert Group on Artificial Intelligence set up by the European Commission[1], EXOSOUL focuses on the individual and proposes a user-driven proactive approach to protect ethics. EXOSOUL recognizes that the human being is unpaired in the digital society and proposes to equip her with a software exoskeleton to make her resilient with respect to potential attacks to her fundamental rights.

References

1. Gartner top 10 strategic technology trends for 2019 (2019). https://gtnr.it/2CJJYGp
2. Autili, M., Inverardi, P., Spalazzese, R., Tivoli, M., Mignosi, F.: Automated synthesis of application-layer connectors from automata-based specifications. J. Comput. Syst. Sci. **104**, 17–40 (2019)
3. Autili, M., Inverardi, P., Tivoli, M.: Automated synthesis of service choreographies. IEEE Softw. **32**(1), 50–57 (2015)

---

[1] https://ec.europa.eu/futurium/en/ai-alliance-consultation/guidelines.

4. Autili, M., Inverardi, P., Tivoli, M.: Choreography realizability enforcement through the automatic synthesis of distributed coordination delegates. Sci. Comput. Program. **160**, 3–29 (2018)
5. Autili, M., Di Ruscio, D., Inverardi, P., Pelliccione, P., Tivoli, M.: A software exoskeleton to protect and support citizen's ethics and privacy in the digital world. IEEE Access **7**, 62011–62021 (2019)
6. Autili, M., Di Salle, A., Tivoli, M.: Synthesis of resilient choreographies. In: Gorbenko, A., Romanovsky, A., Kharchenko, V. (eds.) SERENE 2013. LNCS, vol. 8166, pp. 94–108. Springer, Heidelberg (2013). https://doi.org/10.1007/978-3-642-40894-6_8
7. Awad, E., et al.: The moral machine experiment. Nature **563**, 59–64 (2018)
8. Floridi, L.: Soft ethics and the governance of the digital. Philos. Technol. **31**(1), 1–8 (2018)
9. Inverardi, P.: The European perspective on responsible computing. Commun. ACM **62**(4), 64–69 (2019)
10. Perucci, A., Autili, M., Tivoli, M.: A multipurpose framework for model-based reuse-oriented software integration synthesis. In: 4th International Workshop on Model-Driven Engineering for Component-Based Software Systems (ModComp), pp. 41–47 (2017)
11. Scoccia, G.L., Ruberto, S., Malavolta, I., Autili, M., Inverardi, P.: An investigation into android run-time permissions from the end users' perspective. In: 5th IEEE/ACM International Conference on Mobile Software Engineering and Systems (MOBILESoft) (2018)
12. Scoccia, G.L., Malavolta, I., Autili, M., Di Salle, A., Inverardi, P.: User-centric android flexible permissions. In: Proceedings of the 39th International Conference on Software Engineering, ICSE, pp. 365–367 (2017)
13. Tivoli, M., Inverardi, P.: Failure-free coordinators synthesis for component-based architectures. Sci. Comput. Program. **71**(3), 181–212 (2008)

Invited Paper

A Distilled Characterization of Resilience and Its Embraced Properties Based on State-Spaces

Jesper Andersson[1], Vincenzo Grassi[2], Raffaela Mirandola[3(✉)],
and Diego Perez-Palacin[1]

[1] Linnaeus University, Växjö, Sweden
{jesper.andersson,diego.perez}@lnu.se
[2] University of Roma Tor Vergata, Rome, Italy
vincenzo.grassi@uniroma2.it
[3] Politecnico di Milano, Milan, Italy
raffaela.mirandola@polimi.it

Abstract. In recent years, we have observed the increasing interest in the system property *resilience*. We ascribe this increasing interest to the rapidly growing number of deployed, complex, socio-technical systems, which are facing uncertainty about changes they are expected to experience during their life-cycle and ways to deal with them. This paper contributes to current resilience research by focusing on the different definitions given for this system property, highlighting the risk that, using different terms in different communities, this contributes to create a "tower of Babel" problem, with the consequent difficulty in exchanging ideas and working together towards a common goal. We adopt an extended definition of dependability to define resilience. Based on that, we identify features of resilient systems, capture properties falling under the resilience umbrella, and define a conceptual framework for resilience characterization including how changes affect the system, strategies to design resilience, and discuss metrics for quantifying resilience at design and runtime.

Keywords: Resilience · Conceptual framework · Strategies and metrics

1 Introduction

The complexity of socio-technical systems together with the need to manage the inherent uncertainties related to anticipated and unanticipated changes in the system's environment, in the user needs and behaviors, and the system itself are the drivers for the increased interest in the notion of *resilience* in the last decade.

The concept of resilience was coined and developed in psychology to describe the human ability to cope with a crisis and to recover from it rapidly. Several

© Springer Nature Switzerland AG 2019
R. Calinescu and F. Di Giandomenico (Eds.): SERENE 2019, LNCS 11732, pp. 11–25, 2019.
https://doi.org/10.1007/978-3-030-30856-8_2

other disciplines adopted the term over the years, including system safety [4], medicine [5] and human organization [2]. A wide-spread use in different disciplines has resulted in a situation where the term has several, sometimes incompatible, meanings. Woods [16] provides a comprehensive analysis of the different nuances of the resilience term.

If we put the magnifier glass on the ICT domain, we find a plethora of related terms that originate from different research communities such as dependability, self-*, safety, and security, for example, resilience, robustness, adaptation, recovery, absorption, and flexibility, often without crisply defined relationships.

The research questions motivating the work reported in this paper are:

- What are the different facets of a system that the different terms intend to capture?
- Are some terms specializations (qualifications) of some other terms?
- Are some of them representing means for attaining a property indicated by another term?

There is a vast body of related work [3,10,12,14–16] that contributes to the general discussion on resilience. Many provide conceptual frameworks, which assist in identifying the current state of the art, relationships among different approaches, and the promising research avenues.

We contribute further in this direction, by distilling and presenting concepts from that current body of works in a unified and concise way. In particular, we use the ideas expressed in [3,10,14] as our starting point. These results of discussions mainly belong to the dependability and self-organizing systems communities. Besides, we also refer to the general discussion reported in [16].

In particular, we leverage on Laprie's definition [10] that defines resilience as an extension of dependability when facing changes. We analyze, classify, and propose:

- a conceptual framework based on the principled definitions of terms that concur with the resilience definition;
- a dynamic characterization of resilience in terms of change types the system has to cope with;
- a characterization of the change types affecting the system resilience;
- a discussion about metrics and strategies to measure and realize resilience.

The paper is organized as follows. Section 2 introduces the proposed conceptual framework and the types of changes impacting the system resilience property, Sect. 3 presents a discussion about existing strategies and metrics for resilience, and Sect. 4 concludes the work.

2   A Conceptual Framework for Characterizing Resilience in ICT Systems

In this section, we introduce and briefly explain terms and concepts that capture essential aspects of the ICT systems resilience discourse. Using a broad definition of *resilience* as a starting point, we characterize resilience using these terms and concepts and describe the basic properties of the change types that affect system resilience.

2.1 Basic Terms and Concepts

Resilience - In the following we conform to the Laprie's definition [10]:

Definition. *Resilience is defined as the persistence of dependability when facing changes.*

This definition refers to the *dependability* concept, which is a fundament in a conceptual framework elaborated over several years within the dependable computing community [3]. It defines dependability as: *"The ability to deliver service that can justifiably be trusted."* or, alternatively: *"The dependability of a system is the ability to avoid service failures that are more frequent and more severe than acceptable."*

From these definitions, it is clear that resilience is a broader concept than dependability due to an increase in the number of event types that may affect the system property. Dependability concerns a system's ability to deliver satisfactory service in the presence of "negative" events, such as, faults and even failures. Resilience is more general as it is concerned with a system's ability to delivering satisfactory service in the presence of *changes*. Changes are not necessarily negative events, for example, in ubiquitous systems where a continuous change in the number and type of interacting entities is a rule rather than an exception.

System and Environment - By *System* we mean a broad notion encompassing hardware and software systems, humans, and the physical world with its natural phenomena in which the software and hardware systems are situated. In the research reported herein, we focus on ICT systems consisting of hardware and software components.

The systems we consider are self-similar or *structured systems* that consists of a collection of interacting components, where each component by itself constitutes a system. This definition is recursively applicable until we reach a decomposition level where further decomposition is not relevant for the given context. Besides interacting with other components that are part of the same system, a system also interacts with systems in the system's *environment*. The observers perspective and context define the system-environment boundary. The system interacts and affects the environment, and it is in the environment that observers may evaluate the system effects on it.

System State - The *system state* is the collection of attributes required for describing a system and its behavior.

Hence, a specific state can be modeled as a vector σ belonging to some n-dimensional state space Σ. This simplified state notion encompasses parameters and attributes characterizing both a system and its environment.

system state space

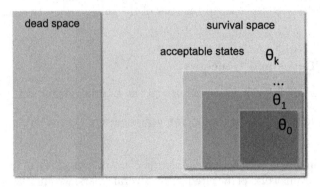

Fig. 1. States classification (adapted from [14]).

State Classification - An *acceptance criterion* θ is a set of constraints and relationships defined on the system state that allows the identification of the subset of the system state space Σ consisting of all those states where the service delivered by the system can be considered correct and acceptable according to θ. We call this subset the set of *acceptable states* with respect to θ, and denote it by $\theta(\Sigma)$.

In general, a number of acceptance criteria $\theta_0, \theta_1, \cdots, \theta_k$ could be defined for a given system, such that $\theta_0(\Sigma) \subseteq \theta_1(\Sigma) \subseteq \cdots \theta_k(\Sigma) \subseteq \Sigma$. The case $k \geq 1$ thus allows considering a series of progressively less stringent acceptance criteria, which can be used in situations where we want to distinguish different levels of more or less degraded but still acceptable performance. Otherwise, the case $k = 0$ represents an on-off situation, where the system state is either acceptable or not acceptable. For a comparison, the discussion in [14] assumes $k = 1$, where $\theta_0(\Sigma)$ and $\theta_1(\Sigma)$ are called *target space* and *acceptable space*, respectively. On the other hand, the discussion in [3] basically assumes $k = 0$, with $\Sigma \setminus \theta_0(\Sigma)$ the set of *error states*.

To fully characterize the system behavior, we introduce two additional subsets of Σ, denoted by $\theta_s(\Sigma)$ and $\theta_d(\Sigma)$, such that $\theta_0(\Sigma) \subseteq \cdots \theta_k(\Sigma) \subseteq \theta_s(\Sigma)$ and $\theta_d(\Sigma) = \Sigma \setminus \theta_s(\Sigma)$. Following [14], we call them the *survival space* and *dead space*, respectively.

The survival space $\theta_s(\Sigma)$ includes all those states where the service delivered by the system may be not acceptable, but for which a sequence of internally or externally initiated corrective actions exists, which bring the system back to a state $\sigma \in \theta_i(\Sigma), 0 \leq i \leq k$. The dead space $\theta_d(\Sigma)$ includes all states where the delivered service is not acceptable and that preclude the possibility of returning to an acceptable state. Figure 1 depicts the state classification.

2.2 A Dynamic Characterization of Resilience

The resiliency definition given in the previous subsection (analogously to the dependability definition from which it is derived) is intended to represent a general and global concept that subsumes several more specific concepts concerning one or more of its facets. In this section, we answer the question: what do we expect from a "resilient system"? Any answer to this question reflects which incarnation of the different resilience concepts it originates from. Further, it will require the adoption of different design and implementation strategies to achieve resilience and the application of different metrics for its measurement.

To this end, we revisit the general definition of resilience using the definitions from the related domains as a prism. Further, we suggest an experimental characterization of the resilience incarnations in terms of system dynamics defined by state transitions and state trajectories.

For a start, the considered resilience definition stresses that it is a property strongly related with the trust we can have in the system ability to remain inside the boundary of some set $\theta_i(\Sigma), 0 \leq i \leq k$, despite the occurrence of events, generically called "changes", that may challenge this ability. Changes are called "disturbances" in [14], and "faults" in [3].

We can distinguish two main kinds of change events that may force a system to cross the boundary of an acceptable states set:

- *"structural changes"*: changes that lead to a modification of the system and/or environment state, denoted as a function $\delta : \Sigma \to \Sigma$. Examples of this kind of events could be a change in the load and/or profile of service requests addressed to a system, a fault of some internal component of the system, the appearance/disappearance of resources in the system environment. Such changes lead to a border crossing if, given a state $\sigma \in \theta_i(\Sigma)$, we have $\delta(\sigma) \notin \theta_i(\Sigma)$.
- *"functional changes"*: changes that lead to a modification of the acceptance criterion, denoted as a function $\rho : \Theta \to \Theta$, where Θ generically denotes the set of possible acceptance criteria. Examples of this kind of events could be a change in the user preferences or requirements, which causes the addition of new criteria, and/or the removal or modification of old criteria. Such changes lead to a border crossing if, given a state $\sigma \in \theta_i(\Sigma)$, we have $\sigma \notin \rho(\theta_i)(\Sigma)$.

We may use these change types to identify several resilience variants. We first consider resilience with respect to a given set **SC** of "structural changes", which could affect a system or its environment. Then, we consider resilience with respect to a given set **FC** of "functional changes".

The proposed resilience classification, with respect to **SC** and a given set of acceptance criteria $\theta_0, \theta_1, \cdots, \theta_k$, depends on which kind of border crossing these changes are able to induce. Besides ideas expressed in [3,14], this classification is also inspired by the discussion in [16].

Definition. *A system is robust with respect to* **SC** *and an acceptance criterion* θ_i, *if for any* $\delta \in$ **SC** *and* $\sigma \in \theta_i(\Sigma)$, *it is* $\delta(\sigma) \in \theta_i(\Sigma)$.

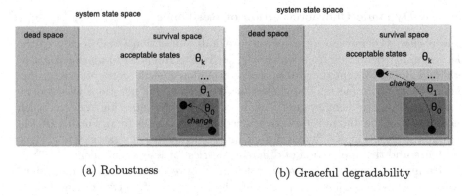

(a) Robustness   (b) Graceful degradability

Fig. 2. Resilience types with acceptable states

This means that a robust system with respect to **SC** never crosses the boundary of the set of acceptable states $\theta_i(\boldsymbol{\Sigma})$. This property is called "strong robustness" in [14], and "robustness" (alias "resilience(2)") in [16]. An illustration of this type of resilience is given in Fig. 2(a).

Definition. *A system is gracefully degradable with respect to **SC** and an acceptance criterion θ_i, with $i < k$, if for any $\delta \in \boldsymbol{SC}$ and $\boldsymbol{\sigma} \in \theta_i(\boldsymbol{\Sigma})$, it is $\delta(\boldsymbol{\sigma}) \in \theta_k(\boldsymbol{\Sigma})$.*

Graceful degradability is thus a weaker property with respect to robustness, however, it retains the idea that the system will always be able to deliver some kind of minimally acceptable service and never enter a non acceptable state. This property is called "weak robustness" in [14], but limited to the case $i = 0$ and $k = 1$. It also partially resembles the "graceful extensibility" (alias "resilience(3)") in [16]. Figure 2(b) depicts the states in case of graceful degradability.

Definition. *A system is recoverable with respect to **SC** and an acceptance criterion θ_i, if for any $\delta \in \boldsymbol{SC}$ and $\boldsymbol{\sigma} \in \theta_i(\boldsymbol{\Sigma})$, it is $\delta(\boldsymbol{\sigma}) \in \theta_k(\boldsymbol{\Sigma}) \cup \theta_s(\boldsymbol{\Sigma})$.*

Recoverability thus implies that the system could temporarily enter states where the delivered service is not acceptable, but has access to sufficient capabilities that enables it to return to an acceptable state by itself or by external control. This property is called "adaptivity/adaptability" in [14]. It is also related to the "rebound" (alias "resilience(1)") property in [16]. This type of resilience is illustrated in Fig. 3(a).

Let us now consider a given set **FC** of "functional changes". We can distinguish some different scenarios:

Definition. *FC is a relaxation of θ_k, when for any $\rho \in \boldsymbol{FC}$ it is:*
$\theta_k(\boldsymbol{\Sigma}) \bigcap \rho(\theta_k)(\boldsymbol{\Sigma}) = \theta_k(\boldsymbol{\Sigma})$.

In this case, a system that is robust/gracefully degradable/recoverable with respect to a given set of "structural changes" **SC** retains the same kind of resilience in the new scenario generated by the introduction of **FC**.

Definition. *FC is a restriction of θ_k, when for any $\rho \in$ **FC** it is:*
$\theta_k(\Sigma) \bigcap \rho(\theta_k)(\Sigma) = \rho(\theta_k)(\Sigma)$.

In this case, a system that is robust for a given set of "structural changes" **SC** loses this resilience property. It cannot guarantee that it can remain within the boundary of the narrower set of acceptable states. On the other hand, a system that is gracefully degradable/recoverable for **SC** retains the same kind of resilience also for the new acceptance criteria defined by **FC**, as it has the built-in capability of maintaining or returning to states where at least a degraded version of **FC** holds.

Definition. *FC is a variation of θ_k when for any $\rho \in$ **FC** it is:*
$\theta_k(\Sigma) \bigcap \rho(\theta_k)(\Sigma) \neq \rho(\theta_k)(\Sigma)$ *and* $\theta_k(\Sigma) \bigcap \rho(\theta_k)(\Sigma) \neq \theta_k(\Sigma)$. *Therefore, a variation introduces a partially or totally new set of acceptance criteria.*

This implies that at least some of the new acceptable states are outside the borders of the old set of acceptable states. In the extreme case, all the new states are outside the borders of the old states, when $\theta_k(\Sigma) \bigcap \rho(\theta_k)(\Sigma) = \emptyset$. As a consequence, in this scenario it does not make sense to try to achieve either robustness or graceful degradation: it is an intrinsic property of this scenario that a given system state that was acceptable before the change caused by **FC** is no longer acceptable (not even as a "degraded" state). The system will thus necessarily experience a permanence in a non-acceptable state for some time. If the system after some time in this condition can change its operations and thereby reach and stay within the new set of acceptable states, the system is resilient to these changes. This behavior resembles *recoverability* discussed above. However, it requires a different kind of capability compared to recoverability. Recoverability realizes the idea that a system always can bounce back to a visited condition, while the scenario we are considering requires a system that is capable of reaching a previously unvisited condition.

Definition. *A system is flexible when it is resilient to FC variations.*

This property is similarly called "flexibility" in [14]. It is also related with the "graceful extensibility" (alias "resilience(3)") and "sustained adaptability" (alias "resilience(4)") properties in [16]. Figure 3(b) illustrates the system state space in the case of flexible systems.

   To conclude this characterization of the resilience concept, we note that our discussion seems to define a hierarchy, with robustness at the top and recoverability and flexibility at the bottom. We want to point out that this hierarchy is only apparent, as it actually holds only under the assumption of an invariant set of changes for all the given definitions; the relative merit of each kind of resilience depends instead on several factors that include, for example, a trade-off among the cost to stay in degraded or non-acceptable states, the cost to provide a system that may never enter these states, and the variety of changes the system is able to cope with. This kind of considerations, where "cost" could encompass several aspects including economic and human, could lead designers to consider

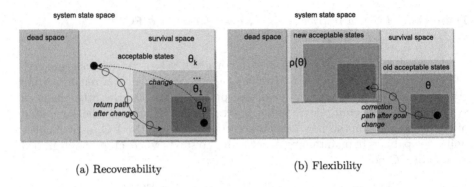

(a) Recoverability   (b) Flexibility

Fig. 3. Resilience types that reach non-acceptable states.

as more viable and effective an apparently weaker kind of resilience. Moreover, as pointed out in [16], we should also consider that the over-provisioning implied by robustness for some set of changes, may lead to increased vulnerability to other changes not included in the set under consideration.

2.3   Basic Properties of Change that Affect the System Resilience

In the previous subsection, we have characterized resilience in terms of inter or intra state-set transitions, triggered by generic "changes" that affect a system. We want to make the characterization more precise to facilitate the assessment of resilience. To this end, we can identify two dimensions, if we study change events from the system perspective: readiness and persistence. These two dimensions are orthogonal to the ones discussed in the previous section.

- the *readiness* of the system to handle a given change; in this case we distinguish between *expected* and *unexpected* changes, and, within the expected, we further distinguish between *handled* and *unhandled* changes;
- the *persistence* of the impact of a given change on the system; in this case we distinguish between *transient* and *permanent* changes.

Figure 4 depicts this classification of changes. We further discuss how this characterization of changes fits into the resilience characterization introduced above.

Expected vs. Unexpected Changes - Expected and handled changes are changes that are part of a system's "normal" operation, in the sense that the system includes hardware and software resources that enable it to manage the changes. These changes include those belonging to the system's nominal behavior, for example, changes in the value read within the working range of a sensor, and "undesired" changes, for example failures. As a consequence, there are no "surprises" (as named in [16]) in this change types. Depending on which design decisions designers make, the system handles these changes differently. Aligned to

Fig. 4. Changes according to the their persistence and readiness to be handled.

the classification presented herein, designers make the system robust, gracefully degradable, or recoverable concerning the changes.

Expected unhandled changes are those changes that are foreseeable and identified, but for which no system provisioning is in place to manage them. The consequence is that if such event occurs, it is likely it brings the system into an unacceptable state, either in the survival $\theta_s(\Sigma)$ or the dead $\theta_d(\Sigma)$ space. Designers may decide not to handle some types of changes during the system development. The rationale for not handling a foreseeable change can be a relatively low occurrence frequency or complicated and costly techniques to introduce system mechanisms that handle the change type. The consequence of these decisions is that the system will lack mechanisms that retain or return the system to an acceptable state automatically. There may however exist protocols that system operators may follow to return the system to an acceptable state.

If there is a protocol for recovering from an identified change, then the change moves the system to a state in the survival space. If there is no such protocol, the change moves the system to a state in the dead space.

If designers do not identify a possible change, it results in possible unexpected changes at runtime, the so-called *surprises*. An unexpected change may move the system to any subspace in the state space, acceptable, survival, or dead spaces. The resilience classification discussed above is not equipped to manage this type of change as it would require a system that can reason about the effect of situations that it is unaware of and possibly identify a protocol for returning the system to an acceptable state. In some cases, the system may already be resilient (robust, gracefully degradable or recoverable, as defined in Sect. 2.2). Apart from these cases, the additional design and development efforts that are required to make the system able to cope with the new type of changes can be reduced if the system has been designed and implemented with a good degree of *flexibility*, as defined in Sect. 2.2, and as remarked also in [16] ("graceful extensibility" (alias "resilience(3)") and "sustained adaptability" (alias "resilience(4)") properties).

Permanent vs. Transient Changes - Following the distinction of fault persistence in [3], we can distinguish two types of change. *Permanent* changes are changes that do not disappear unless some corrective action takes place. *Transient* changes are changes where the system eventually returns to an acceptable state without taking any action. An example of transient change is a power outage that affects a network router. When the power comes back, the router returns to function. Another example is when a software component fails to establish a connection to a database due to multiple concurrent requests. When the load decreases, the component may connect to the database. An example of permanent change is the addition of a new system requirement to be satisfied that is not covered by the existing ones.

When a designer identifies a transient change, the decision of whether handling it or not is a tradeoff between the cost and occurrence of the effect, and the cost of handling the change. If the change is unhandled, the system is intrinsically recoverable (as defined in Sect. 2.2) for the change, with a recovery period duration that corresponds to the duration of the change. A system should always handle permanent changes; that is, it should to be resilient for such changes.

3   Design Strategies and Metrics for Resilience in ICT Systems

Resilience introduces many challenges from a design and implementation perspective. In this section, we briefly discuss strategies for enabling resilience in a system and resilience metrics and measurement strategies for design time and runtime.

3.1   Resilience Strategies

In this section we briefly discuss strategies that achieve the kinds of resilience characterized in Sect. 2.

Resilience as Robustness: We may achieve this property by utilizing *redundancy* techniques. These do not require explicit detection mechanisms for the occurrence of changes or mechanisms that identify the change type (e.g., fault masking using parallel active redundancy with majority voting).

An alternative strategy is *intrinsic algorithmic and structural* system properties that can manage the change within the system's "normal flow" of events. One example of such systems is the self-organizing systems [7] that do not require a mechanism that detects the occurrence of a change.

A third strategy is *proactive (self-)adaptation* that uses forecasting to anticipate possible changes before their occurrence and enacts corrective actions that prevent undesired state changes; as a consequence, these latter techniques do require the identification of the type of change will occur;

Resilience as Graceful Degradability: This is another property where designers may utilize *redundancy* techniques. These techniques are different from the techniques discussed above for robustness, but they have the same advantages of not requiring explicit detection and identification of a change occurrence (e.g., a servers cluster that continues to work at reduced capacity when some server fails, irrespective of the actual cause of server failure).

An alternative strategy is *reactive (self-)adaptation* that in this instance, identifies the change that has occurred and adapts the service or service quality.

For example, a video streaming service detects a change in the available bandwidth and reduces the frame rate to be able to continue the service delivery;

Resilience as Recoverability: The recoverability property is generally achieved utilizing *reactive (self-)adaptation* techniques, which span commoditized techniques like checkpoint-rollback-recovery in database systems and alternative strategies based on, for example, machine-learning methodologies to identify a suitable adaptation plan that restores the system to a correct operational status;

Resilience as Flexibility: There are no well-established strategies for a general flexibility property. Flexibility requires that large parts of a system's behavior change and are verified dynamically. Such radical behavioral changes require a holistic approach that enables online behavior to utilize offline automated development techniques [1]. The practical implications of this strategy are, however, not sufficiently studied. Three critical factors for this strategy are: model availability, tool-chain automation, and decision-making.

Model-availability and the model-quality are essential for a successful realization of general flexibility. The automated tool-chain and decision making mechanisms such as comparisons and reasoning require that the models, which describe the system, are readily available, accurate, and updated. Flexibility also requires that the tools that work on the models are fully automated and configured in tool-chains that reflects development work-flows. An illustration of one such tool-chain is a continuous integration-deployment pipe-line. We conjecture that general flexibility, in some instances, requires updates to the models, tools, and tool-chains in response to radical changes. This meta-adaptation level is currently uncharted territory in research. The final corner-stone in a general flexibility mechanism is support for decision-making. Flexibility requires identification of new acceptable states, generation of correct behavior for the new state-space, and the verification of overall system behavior. This complex process involves several decision types that require support from different reasoning and comparisons strategies for evaluating alternatives, ranking, and decision selection. For example, flexibility may require that the system provides for dynamic assurances, that is assurance structures that describe and argue for the fulfillment of a specific system property. We conjecture that systems with flexibility must be able to communicate and explain the rationale for the decisions it makes. One example of research in this direction is explainable Artificial Intelligence [9].

3.2 Resilience Metrics

The critical role resilience plays in ICT systems elevates the importance of metrics and indicators that provide a quantitative evaluation of resilience. These metrics assist designers and other decision-making stakeholders in obtaining an understanding of a system's resilience status. Hence, they are better prepared to identify, plan, and prioritize activities that improve system resilience. In the past, several efforts have addressed this area and proposed several approaches. We outline some issues concerning the definition of suitable metrics below, distinguishing between *runtime* and *design time* metrics.

Runtime Metrics. Runtime metrics measure to what extent a system is resilient to changes that occur during its operational life. Referring to the resilience characterization given in Sect. 2.2, these metrics are observation-based; that is, they monitor the system's operational state trajectories. The trajectories may visit different parts of the system's state space. With these mechanisms in place, we may collect information and express system resilience in terms of whether or not it has visited a state space, and if so the duration of the visit and which states it visited in $\theta_i(\Sigma)$, for some $i \in \{0, 1, \cdots, k\}$, or in $\theta_s(\Sigma)$ or $\theta_d(\Sigma)$.

As a consequence, we conjecture that runtime metrics are best suited to assess the system resilience for expected changes as the evaluation require at least a partial knowledge of the system dynamics before, during and after a change occurs.

We describe several runtime metrics below that are useful for the different instantiations of the general resilience concept in Sect. 2.2.

- metrics that measure the *continuity* of correct service can be used to asses the robustness of the system; referring to the dependability domain, metrics of this kind are those measuring the system *reliability* (e.g., mean time to failure (MTTF), or probability of never leaving some $\theta_i(\Sigma)$ in some time interval $[0, T]$, where T is the length of the system mission time);
- metrics that measure the *readiness* for correct service can be used to asses the recoverability of the system; referring to the dependability domain, metrics of this kind are those measuring the system *availability* (e.g., ratio of time spent in acceptable states with respect to the total length of the observation interval);
- metrics that measure the *overall accumulated "quality"* of the delivered service can be used to assess the degradability of the system; referring to the dependability domain, metrics of this kind are those measuring the system *performability* (e.g., average quality accumulated in a time interval, assuming that different quality levels are associated with states in different sets $\theta_i(\Sigma)$).

These metrics could then be evaluated starting from the definition of the following quantity:

$$\mu(T) = \int_0^T f(\boldsymbol{\sigma}(t))dt \tag{1}$$

where T denotes the system observation time (it could also be $T = \infty$), $\boldsymbol{\sigma}(t)$ denotes the system state at time t, and $f : \Sigma \to \Re$ is a function that maps the system state space to the set of real numbers. By suitably defining $f(\boldsymbol{\sigma})$ (e.g., in the simplest case, as the indicator function that holds 1 when $\boldsymbol{\sigma} \in \theta_i(\Sigma)$, and 0 otherwise) we can thus use $\mu(T)$ to get measures based on the system states history.[1] A summary of resilience metrics defined in this way can be found in [11].

---

[1] If the system dynamics is described by means of some stochastic model, $\mu(T)$ is a random variable, whose moments or probability distribution can be used as actual resilience metrics.

Design Time Metrics. A design-time resilience metric provides a measure of to what extent the system design makes it prone to structural or behavioral modifications. As a consequence, we argue that design time metrics are best suited to assess the system resilience to unexpected changes, as they do not require apriori knowledge of the system dynamics when these changes occur. The resilience characterization in Sect. 2 points out one type, flexibility, to manage unexpected changes. Hence, design metrics in general targets resilience by flexibility.

The flexibility property is in many aspects similar to the software architecture properties adaptability and extensibility. Eden and Mens [8], propose a reference framework to measure software flexibility, where they adopt a view in which they define complexity from different points of views and consider it as the antipole of flexibility. Besides, they describe a set of indices that can be used to this end and provide a classification of available design paradigms and design patterns well-aligned with their flexibility metrics. Other works, for instance, Cossentino et al. [6] define flexibility and extensibility metrics using classical coupling and cohesion software. The software product line community has defined extensibility metrics. Based on an analysis of the features in a product-line, they have developed some feasible quantitative indicators for extensibility. More recently, as a result of the increasing interest in self-adapting systems, we have seen adaptivity metrics [13] based on the availability of equivalent components on the market for a given application.

4   Discussion and Future Works

Our primary motivation for the work reported herein is to bring structure to the general concept of resilience. Resilience is used and defined in many related knowledge areas in the ICT domain, which has resulted in a multitude of terms and definitions with unclear semantics. A universal nomenclature with well-defined semantics will nourish research in several domains, which will contribute new knowledge to an area that is a corner-stone in modern ICT systems.

To this end, we propose a structure with four types of resilience that manage structural and functional changes in different ways: robustness, graceful degradability, recoverability, and flexibility. The structure forms a basis for a conceptual framework and a dynamic characterization of each resilience type. Besides, we briefly discuss alternative design strategies and design-time and runtime metrics that enable quantitative assessment of the resilience types and corresponding strategies.

Among the resilience types included in the proposed framework, *flexibility* is probably the type that deserves the most attention in the future. Flexibility targets change types that developers are not able to anticipate, identify, and handle. We may, however, require that the system is resilient to these unexpected changes ("surprises"), which is the most intriguing and most demanding system property according to Woods [16]. We conjecture that *flexibility* requires a concerted interdisciplinary research effort that tackles challenging research avenues such as, among others, model availability and quality, tool-chain automation and adaptation, and decision-making and explainability.

More specifically, we plan to investigate some specific areas such as:

1. Strategies and metrics for surprises.
2. Artificial intelligence-based strategies for system resilience.
3. Architectural patterns and tactics for flexibility.
4. Design-time and runtime metrics that capture facets of resilience.
5. A reasoning framework for engineering resilient ICT systems.

In pursuing these lines of research, we plan to adopt a multidisciplinary approach and bring in knowledge areas outside of ICT and leverage advances in, for instance, biology, psychology, and social sciences when tackling the challenges above.

Acknowledgments. Raffaela Mirandola has been partially supported by the *Swedish KK-Stiftelsens* project No. *KKS - 20170232.*

References

1. Andersson, J., et al.: Software engineering processes for self-adaptive systems. In: de Lemos, R., Giese, H., Müller, H.A., Shaw, M. (eds.) Software Engineering for Self-Adaptive Systems II. LNCS, vol. 7475, pp. 51–75. Springer, Heidelberg (2013). https://doi.org/10.1007/978-3-642-35813-5_3
2. Annarelli, A., Nonino, F.: Strategic and operational management of organizational resilience: current state of research and future directions. Omega **62**(C), 1–18 (2016)
3. Avizienis, A., Laprie, J.-C., Randell, B., Landwehr, C.E.: Basic concepts and taxonomy of dependable and secure computing. IEEE Trans. Dependable Secure Comput. **1**(1), 11–33 (2004)
4. Bergström, J., van Winsen, R., Henriqson, E.: On the rationale of resilience in the domain of safety: a literature review. Reliab. Eng. Syst. Saf. **141**, 131–141 (2015). Special Issue on Resilience Engineering
5. Braithwaite, J., Wears, R., Hollnagel, E.: Resilient health care: turning patient safety on its head. Int. J. Qual. Health Care **27**, 08 (2015)
6. Cossentino, M., Lodato, C., Lopes, S., Ribino, P., Palermo, V.: Metrics for evaluating modularity and extensibility in HMAS systems. In: Proceedings of the 2015 International Conference on Autonomous Agents and Multiagent Systems, AAMAS 2015, Richland, SC, pp. 1061–1069. International Foundation for Autonomous Agents and Multiagent Systems (2015)
7. Marzo Serugendo, G.: Robustness and dependability of self-organizing systems - a safety engineering perspective. In: Guerraoui, R., Petit, F. (eds.) SSS 2009. LNCS, vol. 5873, pp. 254–268. Springer, Heidelberg (2009). https://doi.org/10.1007/978-3-642-05118-0_18
8. Eden, A., Mens, T.: Measuring software flexibility. IEE Proc. - Softw. **153**, 113–125 (2006)
9. Gunning, D.: Explainable artificial intelligence (XAI). Defense Advanced Research Projects Agency (DARPA), nd Web, 2 (2017)
10. Laprie, J.-C.: From dependability to resilience. In: DSN 2008 (2008)
11. Najarian, M., Lim, G.J.: Design and assessment methodology for system resilience metrics. Risk Analysis. https://onlinelibrary.wiley.com/doi/abs/10.1111/risa.13274

12. Patriarca, R., Bergström, J., Gravio, G.D., Costantino, F.: Resilience engineering: current status of the research and future challenges. Saf. Sci. **102**, 79–100 (2018)
13. Perez-Palacin, D., Mirandola, R., Merseguer, J.: On the relationships between QoS and software adaptability at the architectural level. J. Syst. Softw. **87**, 1–17 (2014)
14. Schmeck, H., Müller-Schloer, C., Çakar, E., Mnif, M., Richter, U.: Adaptivity and self-organization in organic computing systems. ACM Trans. Auton. Adapt. Syst. **5**(3), 10:1–10:32 (2010)
15. Wiig, S., Fahlbruch, B.: Exploring Resilience: A Scientific Journey from Practice to Theory. Springer, Heidelberg (2019). https://doi.org/10.1007/978-3-030-03189-3
16. Woods, D.D.: Four concepts for resilience and the implications for the future of resilience engineering. Reliab. Eng. Syst. Saf. **141**, 5–9 (2015). Special Issue on Resilience Engineering

Resilience Engineering in Complex
and Critical Applications

Modelling Autonomous Resilient Multi-robotic Systems

Inna Vistbakka[1]([✉]) [iD] and Elena Troubitsyna[1,2]

[1] Åbo Akademi University, Turku, Finland
inna.vistbakka@abo.fi
[2] KTH – Royal Institute of Technology, Stockholm, Sweden
elenatro@kth.se

Abstract. Resilience is an ability of the system to deliver its services in a dependable way despite the changes. In this paper, we propose a multi-agent based formal outlook on ensuring resilience of multi-robotic systems. We represent system functions as collaborative activities performed by the agents with different capabilities. Changes invoke either structural reconfigurations – forming different collaborations or compensative activities – introducing into the system agents with additional capabilities. We formalize the resilience mechanisms and demonstrate their use by a case study – a coordination of a swarm of drones.

1 Introduction

Resilience is an ability of the system to deliver its services in a dependable way despite the changes [15]. The changes might be internal, i.e., caused by the failures of the system components or external – unexpected changes in the operating environment of the system. In both cases, the system should cope with them by reconfiguring itself to enable delivery of its services in a dependable way.

In this paper, we adopt a multi-agent view for reasoning about system resilience. Namely, with each component – agent – of the system we associate a set of functional capabilities. System functions are defined as collaborations of agents. This is a suitable formalisation because it allows us to establish a correspondence between the capabilities required for a dependable function provisioning and capabilities of operational (i.e., not failed and available) agents. The changes in the environment can also be modelled as the demands for certain capabilities.

Such a formalisation offers a suitable basis for modelling different resilience mechanisms. On the one hand, we can define the structural resilience mechanisms, i.e., forming the new collaborations corresponding to the dependability requirements as well as current system and environment state. On the other hand, we can define the compensating resilience mechanisms, i.e., introducing new agents and agent capabilities into the system.

Reasoning about resilience is a complex task that requires a formal basis. In this paper, we rely on Event-B [1] and the associated Rodin Platform [2] as

© Springer Nature Switzerland AG 2019
R. Calinescu and F. Di Giandomenico (Eds.): SERENE 2019, LNCS 11732, pp. 29–45, 2019.
https://doi.org/10.1007/978-3-030-30856-8_3

our formal automated framework. The formalism allows us to define the complex interactions between agents at different levels of abstraction. It supports correct-by-construction development paradigm, which enables a derivation of a resilient system architecture in a number of correctness-preserving refinement steps. We rely on formal specification and refinement in Event-B to define and verify the properties of complex agent collaborations and derive the corresponding agent collaborative and resilience mechanisms.

To demonstrate an application of the proposed formal framework, we present a case study – a coordination of a resilient swarm of drones. We demonstrate how the proposed formalisation can facilitate introducing the patterns for coping with drone failures and environment changes. It allows us to rigorously define resilience mechanisms at different levels of abstraction.

2   Modelling and Refinement in Event-B

Event-B is a state-based formal approach that promotes the correct-by-construction development paradigm and formal verification by theorem proving. In Event-B, a system model is specified using the notion of an *abstract state machine* [1]. An abstract state machine encapsulates the model state, represented as a collection of variables, and defines operations on the state, i.e., it describes the dynamic behaviour of a modelled system. The important system properties that should be preserved are defined as model invariants. Usually a machine has the accompanying component, called context. A context is the static part of a model and may include user-defined carrier sets, constants and their properties (defined as model axioms).

The system dynamic behaviour is described by a collection of atomic *events* defined in a machine part. Generally, an event has the following form:

$$\text{event}_e \;\widehat{=}\; \textbf{any}\; x_e\; \textbf{where}\;\; G_e\; \textbf{then}\; R_e\; \textbf{end}$$

Here event_e is the unique event's name, x_e is the list of local variables, and G_e is the event guard – a predicate over the model state. The body of an event is defined by a *multiple* (possibly nondeterministic) assignment to the system variables. In Event-B, this assignment is semantically defined as the next-state relation R_e. The event guard defines the conditions under which the event is *enabled*, i.e., its body can be executed. If several events are enabled at the same time, any of them can be chosen for execution nondeterministically.

System development in Event-B is based on a top-down refinement-based approach. A development starts from an abstract specification that nondeterministically models the most essential functional system behaviour. In a sequence of refinement steps, we gradually reduce nondeterminism and introduce detailed design decisions. In particular, we can add new events, refine old events as well as replace abstract variables by their concrete counterparts. The *gluing invariants* are used to link the abstract and concrete state variables. A correct refinement ensures that the abstract system's properties are preserved in the concrete one.

The consistency of Event-B models – verification of model well-formedness, invariant preservation as well as correctness of refinement steps – is demonstrated by discharging the relevant proof obligations. Rodin platform [2] provides tool support for modelling and verification in Event-B. In particular, it automatically generates all required proof obligations and attempts to discharge them. When the proof obligations cannot be discharged automatically, the user can attempt to prove them interactively using a collection of available proof tactics.

3   Autonomous Behaviour of a Resilient Multi-robotic System

Multi-robotic systems belong to a large class of distributed systems composed of asynchronously communicating heterogeneous components. In our work we particularly focus on studying a behaviour of multi-robotic systems that should function autonomously, i.e., without human intervention. Such a kind of systems are often deployed in hazardous areas, e.g., disaster areas, minefields, remote locations, etc. Typically, the autonomic aspect assumes that a system is able to monitor its behaviour and dynamically adapt it, if needed. From the resilience perspective, system autonomy of multi-robotic systems can be achieved via dynamic reconfiguration.

Essentially, a system configuration is a specific arrangement of the elements (components) that compose the system [21]. A configuration can be defined by relationships and dependencies between system elements that are established to support achieving system missions. In its turn, dynamic reconfiguration implies that the system is capable to evolve from its current configuration to another one. Dynamic system reconfiguration may imply substitution, introducing new, or even removal of configurable components, which consequently leads to changing of interdependencies between components. Reconfiguration may also affect component interactions. The purpose of reconfiguration is to ensure that the system remains operational, i.e., enables delivery of services in a dependable way [21].

In our work, we adopt the *agent-based paradigm* to demonstrate how to reason about collaborative component activities and resilience of component interactions. We view the system components as agents and the overall system as a multi-agent system, correspondingly. Next we present our reasoning on resilience-explicit modelling of agent interactions in multi-agent systems.

3.1   Resilience-Explicit Modelling of Multi-agent Interactions

In this section we present a formal reasoning about a resilient multi-agent system. In particular, we introduce agents, their attributes and as well as agent relationships and interactions. The formalisation allows us to establish logical connections between agents and define the conditions under which agent interactions result in correct execution of a cooperative activity to ensure system resilience. The established dynamic relationships between agents allow us to reason about resilience of complex agent interactions.

Definition 1. *A multi-agent system* $\mathcal{MAS}$ *is a tuple* $(\mathsf{A}, \mathsf{C}, \mathsf{R}, \mathsf{Active}, \mathsf{Rel})$, *where*

- A *is a set of all the system agents,*
- C *is a set of agent capabilities,*
- R *is a set of all possible relationships between agents in a* $\mathcal{MAS}$.
- *Moreover, the dynamic system attribute* Active *defines a set of the active (healthy) system agents and the dynamic attribute* Rel *defines a set of dynamic relationships between the agents.*

We call *active* those agents which can carry out the tasks in order to achieve the system missions. In its turn, *inactive* agents are those agents that are not currently in the system or those that are failed and thus incapable to carry out any tasks.

The dynamic system attribute Rel defines dynamic relationships – logical connections – between agents. Several system agents being in a dynamic relationship means that these agents might be or are currently engaged in a certain collaboration required to provide a predefined system function.

We assume that a system consists of a number of agents with different functionalities (capabilities). The agents utilise their capabilities in order to achieve the system missions. For each agent, we can define the set of its capabilities as a structure AC:

$$\forall \, a_i : a_i \in \mathsf{A} \Rightarrow \mathsf{AC}(a_i) \subseteq \mathsf{C}.$$

All possible environment changes as well as agent failures make their capabilities unavailable. Thus agent capabilities AC is a dynamic structure, i.e., during system execution a set of current agent capabilities might vary.

AC represents a partitioning of the system agents into different groups according to their capabilities. We can also define agent classes, where each system agent belongs to a particular agent class. In general, there can be many agent classes A_i, $i \in 1..n$, such that $\mathsf{A}_i \subseteq \mathsf{A}$.

All possible dynamic relationships between system agents of the same or different classes are define in R. We can additionally assume that there are a number of data constructor functions to create elements of R (similarly as we proposed in our work [21]). Any relationship $r \in \mathsf{R}$, r can be modelled as a result of an application of some data constructor function

$$r = \mathsf{R\_Constr}_r(a_1, a_2, \ldots, a_m),$$

where $\mathsf{R\_Constr}_r : \mathsf{A}^*_{i_1} \times \mathsf{A}^*_{i_2} \times \ldots \times \mathsf{A}^*_{i_m} \rightarrowtail \mathsf{R}$. Here m, $m \in \mathbb{N}$, defines a number of agents participating in a relation r and each $\mathsf{A}^*_{i_j} = \mathsf{A}_k \cup \{?\}$ for some agent type A_k. Moreover, $\rightarrowtail$ symbol designates an injection function and "?" stands for an unknown agent of the corresponding class.

We distinguish between two types of relationships: *pending* (i.e., incomplete) and *resolved* (complete). Pending relationships are often caused by a failure or disappearance of the agents previously involved in a relationship. Moreover, an existing active agent may initiate a new pending relationship. A pending relation is marked by putting the question marks instead of a concrete agent (e.g., $R\_Constr_r(a_1, ?, a_3, ?, a_5)$). As soon as a pending relationship is resolved, the question mark is replaced by a concrete agent (similarly, as we did in [21]).

R represents all possible agent relationships and Rel stores the currently active (both pending and complete) relationships. For a relationship to be active, all the involved in it agents should be active as well. In other words, if a concrete agent a_i is involved in r, it should be an active one, i.e., $a_i \in$ Active.

Next we formulate a number of required properties that should be preserved for correct agents interactions.

Property 1. Let EAA be all interaction activities defined between agents and let EA_l be all local agent activities. Moreover, for each agent $a \in A$, let $E(a)$ be a set of activities in which the agent a can be involved. Then

$$\forall a \cdot a \in \text{Active} \Rightarrow E(a) \in \text{EAA} \cup \text{EA}_l \quad and \quad \forall a \cdot a \notin \text{Active} \Rightarrow E(a) \in \text{EA}_l.$$

This property regulates agent interactions with respect to the agent health status. For example, this property implies that when an agent has failed, it cannot be involved into any cooperative activities with other agents. Therefore, while modelling agent interactions, we have to take into account the agent status.

Now we will briefly discuss how the notions defined above can be transferred and incorporated into an Event-B model. We introduce static system notions (such as A, C, etc.) as sets and constants in a model context and define their properties as a number of context axioms. Dynamic system attributes (such as Active, Rel, etc.) are formalised as model variables in a machine part.

Then, in the machine part, we define events modelling agent local activities – joining and leaving the system. Those activities are modelled by the corresponding events Activation and Deactivation:

```
Activation ≘
  any a
  where a ∈ A ∧ a ∉ Active
  then Active := Active ∪ {a}
  end

Deactivation ≘
  any a
  where a ∈ Active
  then Active := Active \ {a}
  end
```

```
Interaction_k ≘
  any a_i, a_j, c_i, c_j
  where a_i ∈ Active ∧ a_j ∈ Active ∧
        c_i ⊆ AC(a_i) ∧ c_j ⊆ AC(a_j) ∧
        Elig_k(c_i, c_j) = TRUE ∧ ...
  then ...
  end
```

The event $Interaction_k$ abstractly models a possible interaction between two agents. Here, in the event guard, we specify conditions when this interaction can happen. We require that only active agents can interact with each other. We additionally assume that each agent should also have a number of capabilities to participate in this interaction. Thus $Elig\_k(c_i, c_j) = TRUE$ abstractly models a specific eligibility condition on the agent capabilities that should be checked before this agent interaction.

The next property concerns collaborative activities between the agents and how these activities are linked with the inter-agent relationships.

Property 2. *Let* EAA *be all the interactions in which active agents may be involved. Moreover, for each active agent* a, *let* R_a *be all the relationships it may be involved in. Finally, for each collaborative activity* ca $\in$ EAA, *let* A_{ca} *be a set of all agents involved in it. Then, for each* ca $\in$ EAA,

$$\bigcap_{a \in A_{ca}} R_a \neq \varnothing.$$

This property regulates the interaction activities between the agents – only the agents that are linked by dynamic relationships can be involved into cooperative activities. In general, some of the relationships might be pending.

In Event-B we can abstractly specify a collaborative activity between two agents by introducing a generic event CollaborativeActivity$_{ca}$. In the event guard we define the conditions on this activity: both agents, participating in a collaboration, are active, eligible to be involved, and there is a pre-existing relationships that permits their interactions:

CollaborativeActivity$_{ca}$ $\widehat{=}$
  any a_i, a_j, c_i, c_j
  where $a_i \in Active \wedge a_j \in Active \wedge$
        $c_i \subseteq AC(a_i) \wedge c_j \subseteq AC(a_j) \wedge$
        $Elig\_ca(c_i, c_j) = TRUE \wedge$
        $R\_Const_{ca}(a_i \mapsto a_j) \in Rel$
  then   ...
  end

Initiation of a new relationship between agents can be specified by the following event InitiateCollaboration$_c$ given below. In the event guards we checked that all the required agents are active, eligible and ready to enter the relationship:

InitiateCollaboration$_c$ $\widehat{=}$
  any a_i, a_j, c_i, c_j
  where $a_i \in Active \wedge a_j \in Active \wedge$
        $c_i \subseteq AC(a_i) \wedge c_j \subseteq AC(a_j) \wedge$
        $Elig\_c(c_i, c_j) = TRUE \wedge ...$
  then $Rel := Rel \cup R\_Const_c(a_i \mapsto a_j)$
      ...
  end

The behaviour modelled by CollaborativeActivity$_{ca}$ and InitiateCollaboration$_c$ events describe generic cases of interactions between agents. Next we will discuss how such agent interactions allow us to build different mechanisms to ensure system resilience.

Modelling Resilience Mechanisms in MAS. The introduced notions and properties discussed above offer a suitable basis for modelling different resilience mechanisms in the context of multi-agent systems. We can define the structural resilience mechanisms (i.e., forming the new collaborations) and the compensating resilience mechanisms (i.e., introducing new agents or capabilities into the system). Moreover, we also can define a simple case of a resilience mechanism – local agent mechanism. Essentially, it is an agent's actions that are performed to deal with local failures or distractions (e.g., obstacle avoidance mechanisms, etc.). Next we will discuss how we can model these mechanisms in Event-B.

A local resilient mechanism can be modelled in Event-B as the following generic event LocalResilientMechanism$_{lm}$ given below. Upon detection a change in system or environment, an agent performs the required remedy actions to tolerate this disturbance. Here we should check that an agent is healthy, has required capabilities and eligible to perform these actions.

```
LocalResilientMechanism_lm ≙
   any  a_i, c_i, d_lm
   where  disturb_condition(d_lm) = TRUE
          a_i ∈ Active ∧ c_i ⊆ AC(a_i) ∧
          Elig_lm(c_i) = TRUE ∧ ...
   then ... // core agent functionality
   end
```

In its turn, reconfiguration mechanism is supported by collaborative agent behaviour, where agent collaborations are regulated by relationships between agents. As we discussed before, we can specify initiation of a new relationship between agents by the event InitiateCollaboration$_c$. However, when some agent of the initiated relationship is still unknown (e.g., should be elected), this situation can be defined by the following event InitiatePendingRelationship$_{pc}$.

```
InitiatePendingRelationship_pc ≙
   any  a_i, c_i
   where  a_i ∈ Active ∧ c_i ⊆ AC(a_i) ∧
          Elig_pc(c_i) = TRUE ∧ ...
   then  Rel := Rel ∪ R_Const_ca(a_i ↦ none)
   ...
   end
```

Here we use the pre-defined element *none* to designate a missing agent in the pending relationship. In this event, an agent a_i initiates a new pending relationship, where the place for a second agent of the particular type is currently vacant (i.e., is marked by *none*). The resulting pending relationships is added to *Rel*.

The pending relationship $R\_Const_{ca}(a_i \mapsto none)$ is resolved, when the corresponding agent "joins" this collaborative activity. The event AcceptRelationship$_{ca}$ abstractly models this situation.

```
AcceptRelationship_ca ≙
   any  a_i, a_j, c_i, c_j
   where   a_i ∈ Active ∧ a_j ∈ Active ∧
           c_i ⊆ AC(a_i) ∧ c_j ⊆ AC(a_j) ∧
           Elig_ca(c_i, c_j) = TRUE ∧
           R_Const_ca(a_i ↦ none) ∈ Rel ∧ ...
   then    Rel := (Rel \ R_Const_ca(a_i ↦ none)) ∪ R_Const_ca(a_i ↦ a_j)
   ...
   end
```

The system reconfiguration mechanisms can be based on reallocation of execution of certain functional tasks from some components (e.g., failed) to the another (e.g., healthy) ones. Such a mechanism guarantees system resilience in the presence of agent failures. If reallocation of agents is required, a reconfiguration can be defined in general case as follows:

$$
\begin{aligned}
&\text{RellocReconfiguration}_r \; \hat{=} \\
&\quad \mathbf{any} \;\; a_i, a_j, a_m, c_i, c_j, c_m \\
&\quad \mathbf{where} \;\; a_i \in Active \wedge a_m \in Active \;\; \wedge \ldots \\
&\qquad\qquad Elig\_r(c_i, c_j, c_m) = TRUE \;\wedge \\
&\qquad\qquad R\_Const_r(a_i \mapsto a_j) \in Rel \;\; \wedge \ldots \\
&\quad \mathbf{then} \;\;\; Rel := (Rel \setminus R\_Const_r(a_i \mapsto a_j)) \;\; \cup \;\; R\_Const_r(a_i \mapsto a_m) \\
&\quad \ldots \\
&\quad \mathbf{end}
\end{aligned}
$$

Let us note, that in a similar way, we can model all collaborating activities involving any number of agents.

Next we will demonstrate an application of the proposed formal framework and present a case study – a coordination of a resilient swarm of drones. We will show how relying on the proposed principles presented in this Section develop a correct system specification. We will discuss the coordination of drones and their collaborative behaviour as well as the resilience aspect of the swarm control. We demonstrate also how refinement process in Event-B can facilitate modelling and verification of inter-tangled agent interactions at different levels of abstraction.

4   Modelling of a Resilient Swarm of Drones

4.1   Case Study Description

Nowadays swarms of drones are rapidly gaining popularity and widely used for surveillance, shipping, rescue etc. In general, a swarm is a distributed system composed of multiple autonomous drones that can be used to accomplish a specific mission. An example of such a mission can be "areal monitoring of a certain area".

The swarms of drones should operate safely, i.e., avoid collisions with each other and unforeseen objects appearing in the flight zones [25]. Moreover, while planning a mission for a swarm, we should determine a balance between the quality of produced payload data by drones and their energy consumption. Essentially, we have to guarantee that the travel distance of the drones is minimised together with the risk of their collision with each other and the unforeseen dynamically appearing objects [26].

A multi-layered architecture of the swarm system [24,26] is presented in Fig. 1(a). The Navigation Coordination Centre (NCC) is responsible for generating the efficient navigation plan according to the mission goals and preventing unsafe behaviour. In our previous work [17,18] we proposed high-performance machine learning and evolutionary algorithms. These algorithms allow NCC to safely navigate the drones and optimise travel distance, resource consumption and quality of payload data ratio. They also ensure collision avoidance between drones as well as between drones and predictable obstacles.

The primary responsibility of Monitoring Centre (MC) is to communicate with the drones and send them the flight routes received from NCC. In their turn, the drones periodically send their payload data (e.g., imaging) and telemetry data (status, position, battery level, etc.) to MC, which sends them to NCC.

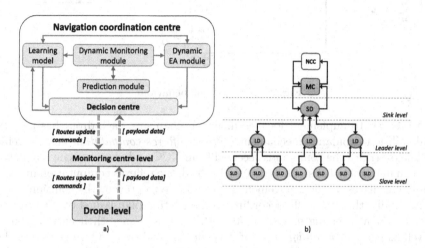

Fig. 1. Overview of a system architecture [24, 26]

Periodically, NCC receives the payload and telemetry data from the drones, analyses this information, and if required, generates a new routing for the entire swarm. Based on received information NCC is able detect the changes in the swarm and in the flying zone. If the required safety level is not reached, NCC invokes recalculation of the drone routes and reconfiguration in the swarm.

During a mission execution drones communicate with each other and MC. Communication with MC is typically long range and might consume significant energy. To solve the problem of fast energy depletion, the swarm of the drones can be organised hierarchically and form a tree-structure depending on its different capabilities: more powerful drones – *the leaders* and less powerful drones – *the slaves* – that communicate with their leaders using less power consuming means. Moreover, a dedicated leader drone – sink drone – establishes communication and transmits data between MC and drones at the leader level. In its turn, the drones of the leader level send data to this sink. Each leader has a number of slave drones and periodically collects information from its slaves. Slaves exchange information with their leaders and might receive new commands generated by NCC. All the layers of the architecture are shown in Fig. 1(b).

During a mission execution some drones might deviate from their predefined routes or even fail. To maintain an efficient drone configuration, NCC periodically assesses the current state of the swarm and might reconfigure the tree.

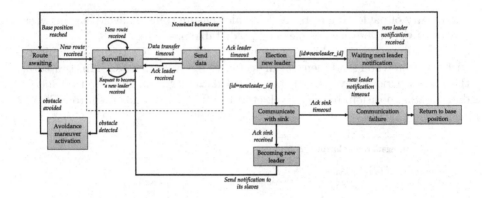

Fig. 2. A slave drone behaviour

Moreover, to implement local resilience mechanisms, each drone has its own local collision avoidance mechanism – *drone reflexes computation module.* This module overrides the commands received from NCC and executes safe maneuver when an unexpected obstacle is detected. The drone reflexes computation module locally calculates a reflex movement for the drone to prevent the collision [26].

Normally, the drones fly according to the routing plan issued by NCC. Periodically, upon receiving new commands the drones change their current routes as well as perform *reconfiguration* if it is commanded by NCC. In this case, the logical relationships between the drones (i.e., *sink-leader* and *leader-slave* relationships) might be changed according to a new update of a drone tree-structure recalculated by NCC.

We distinguish different cases of behaviour of a collaborative swarm of drones at every architectural level (for more details see [24]):

- When a drone (of any layer) detects a possible collision with an unforeseen obstacle or other drone, its reflexes computation module quickly computes a reflex movement to avoid the collision.
- If MC detects a sink failure, MC triggers a reconfiguration to substitute the failed sink drone by the predefined drone among the leaders. In case, if any leader drone detects a sink failure before MC does it, the similar reconfiguration procedure is triggered to substitute the failed sink drone.
- In case of a leader failure, detectable by the sink, the sink drone tries to re-establish connection with the failed leader drone and, in case of unsuccessful outcome considers this leader as failed. The reconfiguration procedure is triggered to substitute the failed leader drone by the predefined slave drone of the failed leader.
- In case of a slave failure, detectable by its leader, the leader drone tries to re-establish connection with the failed slave drone. If it fails, then the failed slave "leaves" the swarm.
- When a drone (of any layer) detects its local communication failure, a drone should try to reconnect with a drone of the upper layer or MC and thus reunite with the swarm.

The described system characterised by complex logic due to the highly non-deterministic nature of the conditions triggering drones behavioural transitions (e.g., see a slave drone state diagram depicted Fig. 2). Ensuring correctness of collaborative behaviour of a swarm of drones is a complex engineering task. Next we demonstrate how Event-B refinement process can facilitate modelling of the multi-layered drone coordination and intertangled drone interactions. Performing this development we apply our modelling principles for a design of a resilient MAS proposed in Sect. 3.

4.2   Event-B Development of a Swarm of Drones

The main focus of our Event-B development is a specification of a complex collaborative behaviour of drones in a swarm-based system. While modelling, we use our formalisation presented in Sect. 3 that covers the notions of system agent, agent capabilities and statuses as well as agent relationships.

Modelling Drones and Their Interdependencies. In our initial specification, we model drones and required relationships between them. Thus we define the elements of the Definition 1. In the context part of our Event-B specification, we represent the swarm by a finite non-empty set of drones *SWARM*. This set might contain the ids of all drones in the swarm. Then we define variables to specify the set of all drones, leaders and slaves drones, as well as the sink drone (by the variables *cur_drones*, *leaders*, *slaves*, *sink*, correspondingly):

$$\{sink\} \cup leaders \cup slaves = cur\_drones, \ cur\_drones \subseteq SWARM.$$

To model the health status of the drones, we introduce a variable *status*. It is defined as a total function:

$$status \in cur\_drones \rightarrow \{OK, FAILED, DISCON\}.$$

Here the constants *OK*, *FAILED* and *DISCON* represent correspondingly the nominal, failed and disconnected drone status. Then, *Active* notion (from the Definition 1) will be represented as a set comprehension:

$$\{a \mid a \in cur\_drones \land status(a) = OK\} = Active.$$

Let us note that we intentionally introduce only drone statuses and partition of all drones and do not introduce the notion of drone's capabilities here. Such an abstraction of drone statuses allows us to avoid introducing all drones capabilities of the different layers and to have only three states covering all the cases that might effect drone functionality and thereby mission achievement.

Next, we define possible relationships between drones, thereby we specify the elements of the system attribute *Rel*. First, *slaves_of_leaders* variable establishes the relationship between a leader and slaves it supervises:

$$slaves\_of\_leaders \in leaders \rightarrow \mathbb{P}(slaves).$$

Here $\rightarrow$ denotes a total function relation, $\mathbb{P}$ denotes powerset of a set.

Moreover, we define *sink_alt* and *leader_alt* variables to model the next sink candidate and leader candidates, respectively.

Performing this modelling step we further apply our modelling rules (properties) proposed in Sect. 3. In the machine part, we specify events to model possible drones failures as well as system reaction on them. We define SINK_Failure, LEADER_Failure and SLAVE_Failure events modelling a permanent failure of the sink, a leader or slave, correspondingly, as well as SINK_discon, LEADER_discon and SLAVE_discon events modelling their transient failures. Upon execution of these events, the value of *status* variable is changed. These events are modelled in the same way as the generic events presented in Sect. 3.

The new event LEADER_Failure_Detection models detection of a sink failure, while SINK_Failure_Reconfiguration event models an election of a "new" sink from one of leader drones. In this case, *slaves_of_leaders* as well as *leaders*, *slaves*, *sink_alt*, *leader_alt* variables are updated. Similarly, new events are introduced to model slave and sink failures as well as the required reconfigurations. An excerpt from this modelling step is presented in Fig. 3.

While our modelling, we formulate and prove the correctness of the reconfiguration mechanisms involving changes all the layers of the architecture. For instance, we prove that no slaves become dispatched from some leader. However, in general, not every leader might have slaves:

$$\forall\ sl.\ sl \in slaves \Rightarrow (\exists\ ld.\ ld \in leaders \wedge sl \in slaves\_of\_leaders(ld)).$$

Modelling Agent Interactions. In next refinement step, we model the remaining agents interactions and, in particular, focus on drones communication model. Communication is a critical aspect in ensuring resilient coordination of the autonomous swarm of drones. The drones communicate with each other to distribute the commands received from MC and NCC and send collected data.

While modelling drones interactions, we should introduce restrictions on these activities to happen, e.g., only the drones that are linked by specific dynamic relationships can be involved in an interaction. The routes transfer is an example of a collaborative activity between two drones of different layers. It can be modelled according to the generic event CollaborativeActivity presented in Sect. 3. In Fig. 4, the event LeaderToSlave_RoutesTransfer models sending new routes from a leader to its corresponding slave drone. The data transmission between all the other layers in the swarm can be modelled in a similar way.

Modelling Local Drone Behaviour. Next we extend our specification by refining it to introduce a drone obstacle avoidance mechanism that contributes to overall system resilience. The event Unpredictable_Obstacle models possibility of appearing an obstacle in a drone flying zone. Then, upon detection an obstacle, a drone computes the best safe position and moves there. This behaviour is covered in the event Reflection_Activation. The nominal behaviour of drone is restored after NCC receives the update about the current drone positions and calculates the new routing for the swarm. To model this required behaviour, we introduce the new event Reunite_Swarm and refine the number of old events (e.g., Update_Local_Routes).

Machine ResilientSwarm_m1   **Sees** ResilientSwarm_c1

Variables $...,$ $cur\_drones,$ $sink,$ $leaders,$ $slaves,$ $status,$ $slaves\_of\_leaders,$ $sink\_alt, ...$

Invariants $... \wedge cur\_drones \subseteq SWARM \wedge leaders \subseteq cur\_drones \wedge$
$\quad slaves \subseteq cur\_drones \ \wedge sink \in cur\_drones \wedge sink\_alt \in cur\_drones \ \wedge ... \wedge$
$\quad slaves\_of\_leaders \in leaders \to \mathbb{P}(slaves) \ \wedge ... \wedge$
$\quad \forall \ sl. \ sl \in slaves \ \Rightarrow \ (\exists \ ld. \ ld \in leaders \ \wedge \ sl \in slaves\_of\_leaders(ld)) \ \wedge$
$\quad status \in cur\_drones \to \{OK, FAILED, DISCON\}$

Events ...

SINK_Failure $\widehat{=}$
  when $status(sink) = OK$
  then $status(sink) := FAILED$
  end

...

SINK_Failure_Reconfiguration $\widehat{=}$
any ld_alt, new_ld_alt, sls
where $... \wedge status(sink)=FAILED \wedge$
  $status(sink\_alt) = OK \wedge sls = slaves\_of\_leader(sink\_alt) \setminus \{ld\_alt\} \wedge$
  $ld\_alt=leader\_alt(sink\_alt) \wedge new\_ld\_alt \in sls$
then
  $sink := sink\_alt$ // new sink is elected
  $sink\_alt := ld\_alt$
  $leaders := (leaders \setminus \{sink\_alt\}) \cup \{ld\_alt\}$
  $slaves := slaves \setminus \{ld\_alt\}$
  $leader\_alt(ld\_alt) := new\_ld\_alt$
  $slaves\_of\_leader := (\{sink\_alt\} \vartriangleleft slaves\_of\_leader) \cup \{ld\_alt \mapsto sls\}$
                                    // slaves sls get new leader
end

...

Fig. 3. The machine ResilientSD_m1

LeaderToSlave_RoutesTransfer $\widehat{=}$ // collaboration for data exchange
any $ld, sl, data$
where $... \wedge status(ld)=OK \wedge status(sl) = OK \wedge$
  $sl \in slaves\_of\_leaders(ld)$ // **representation of** $RConst_i(a1 \mapsto a2) \in Rel$
  $routes :\in ROUTES \ \wedge routes = routes\_for\_slaves(ld \mapsto sl) \in ...$
then
    $cur\_routes(sl) = routes$
    ...
end

Fig. 4. The event LeaderToSlave_RoutesTransfer

5   Conclusions and Related Work

In this paper, we have proposed a formal approach to development of resilient multi-robotic systems. We have proposed a multi-agent based formalisation of reasoning about system resilience by introducing the notions of collaborations and capabilities. It has allowed us to rigorously define different resilience mechanisms and facilitate the design of system reconfiguration as the main mechanism for achieving system resilience.

In this paper, we have also demonstrated the application of the proposed formalisation to the development of a resilient multi-robotic system – a swarm of drones. Our approach allowed us to rigorously define the reconfiguration mechanisms at different levels of abstraction in a swarm. It facilitated the development of complex reconfiguration procedures and deriving the associated coordination mechanisms.

In this paper, we relied on formal modeling and verification in Event-B and associated Rodin platform. Event-B adopts proof-based approach to verification. We believe that it is a promising direction in formal modelling and verification of multi-robotic systems, since it allows us to achieve scalability both in terms of the number of the agents as well as reconfiguration scenarios. The automated tool support – Rodin platform – facilitated derivation of complex system architecture in a disciplined structured way.

In this paper, we have taken a qualitative logic view on system resilience and focused on development and verification of different resilience mechanism. As a future work, it would be interesting to combine the proposed approach with quantitative stochastic reasoning [23]. This would enable not only design but also the assessment of different reconfiguration strategies as well as different system resilience attributes.

Autonomous systems, such as unmanned aerial and marine vehicles, robotic and drone systems, have been widely studied from different perspectives in the software engineering community. In particular, a great number of research in autonomous robotic systems has focused on a development of underling system architectures, robot control and navigation [5,12,16].

A variety of software engineering techniques and tools are used to design dependable robotic systems [16,22,27], including model-checking [13], theorem proving techniques [19], runtime verification [8], simulation [30], etc. Winfield et al. [28] used a linear temporal logic (LTL) to formally specify and verify the behaviour of a swarm robotic system performing aggregation.

A formal verification approach for the design of collective robotic systems is discussed in [10]. In this work the formal language Klaim and related analysis tools are used to model aspects of both the robot hardware and behaviour, as well as relevant aspects of the environment. In our approach we do not only derive an architecture of controlling software of a swarm of drones but also verify motion safety properties of drone navigation.

MAS represents a popular paradigm for modelling complex and distributed systems. Various methodologies and tools have been proposed for design, development and verification of MAS: AUML [3], Gaia [29], MaSE [7], ADELFE [4],

Tropos [6], etc. However these approaches are limited to provide rigorous reasoning about agent behaviour as well as agent interactions. In our work we attempt to formally model each individual agent as well as the dynamic behaviour of the overall system. Moreover, employed Event-B modelling method was capable of rigorously describing all the essential aspects of collaborative behaviour in MAS.

Similar to our work, Ferber et al. [9] propose a set of general principles from which MAS may be designed (in particular, for capturing the organisational structure of MAS). However, our formalisation covers a more wide range of aspects of MAS and agent behaviour (agents capabilities, statuses, relationships, interactions, etc.).

The cooperative motion and task planning scheme for MAS is discussed in [11]. The presented approach is applicable to MAS where the agents have independently assigned local tasks. In contrast, in our work we consider cooperative agent behaviour, where an agent might take responsibility for a specific task depending on its available capabilities.

Reconfiguration in MAS is studied also in work [20]. In this work, the reconfiguration is triggered as soon as real-time requirements are not satisfied (e.g., a certain deadline for task accomplishment is expired). In contrast, in our approach, reconfiguration is triggered as soon as changes in system and its environment violate safety issues associated with a system behaviour.

In our formalisation we focused on providing the logical reasoning of the relationships between agents, their interactions and dynamic reconfiguration. However, we still have abstracted away from some features that could be interesting to study in the future. As a possible future direction, it would be interesting to combine the presented approach with the resilient-explicit goal-oriented refinement process that we proposed in [14]. In this work, the goal-oriented framework provided us with a suitable basis for reasoning about reconfigurability. Combined view would allow us to define reconfigurability as an ability of agents to redistribute their responsibilities via correct interactions and collaborations to ensure goal reachability. The resulting formal systematisation can be used then as generic guidelines for formal development of reconfigurable systems.

References

1. Abrial, J.R.: Modeling in Event-B. Cambridge University Press, Cambridge (2010)
2. Abrial, J., Butler, M.J., Hallerstede, S., Hoang, T.S., Mehta, F., Voisin, L.: Rodin: an open toolset for modelling and reasoning in Event-B. STTT 12(6), 447–466 (2010). https://doi.org/10.1007/s10009-010-0145-y
3. Bauer, B., Müller, J.P., Odell, J.: Agent UML: a formalism for specifying multi-agent software systems. Int. J. Softw. Eng. Knowl. Eng. 11(3), 207–230 (2001). https://doi.org/10.1142/S0218194001000517
4. Bernon, C., Gleizes, M.-P., Peyruqueou, S., Picard, G.: ADELFE: a methodology for adaptive multi-agent systems engineering. In: Petta, P., Tolksdorf, R., Zambonelli, F. (eds.) ESAW 2002. LNCS, vol. 2577, pp. 156–169. Springer, Heidelberg (2003). https://doi.org/10.1007/3-540-39173-8_12

5. Brambilla, M., Ferrante, E., Birattari, M., Dorigo, M.: Swarm robotics: a review from the swarm engineering perspective. Swarm Intell. **7**(1), 1–41 (2013). https://doi.org/10.1007/s11721-012-0075-2

6. Bresciani, P., Perini, A., Giorgini, P., Giunchiglia, F., Mylopoulos, J.: Tropos: an agent-oriented software development methodology. Auton. Agents Multi-Agent Syst. **8**(3), 203–236 (2004). https://doi.org/10.1023/B:AGNT.0000018806.20944.ef

7. DeLoach, S.A.: Multiagent systems engineering of organization-based multiagent systems. ACM SIGSOFT Softw. Eng. Notes **30**(4), 1–7 (2005). https://doi.org/10.1145/1082983.1082967

8. Falcone, Y., Jaber, M., Nguyen, T.-H., Bozga, M., Bensalem, S.: Runtime verification of component-based systems. In: Barthe, G., Pardo, A., Schneider, G. (eds.) SEFM 2011. LNCS, vol. 7041, pp. 204–220. Springer, Heidelberg (2011). https://doi.org/10.1007/978-3-642-24690-6_15

9. Ferber, J., Gutknecht, O., Michel, F.: From agents to organizations: an organizational view of multi-agent systems. In: Giorgini, P., Müller, J.P., Odell, J. (eds.) AOSE 2003. LNCS, vol. 2935, pp. 214–230. Springer, Heidelberg (2004). https://doi.org/10.1007/978-3-540-24620-6_15

10. Gjondrekaj, E., et al.: Towards a formal verification methodology for collective robotic systems. In: Aoki, T., Taguchi, K. (eds.) ICFEM 2012. LNCS, vol. 7635, pp. 54–70. Springer, Heidelberg (2012). https://doi.org/10.1007/978-3-642-34281-3_7

11. Guo, M., Dimarogonas, D.V.: Multi-agent plan reconfiguration under local LTL specifications. I. J. Robot. Res. **34**(2), 218–235 (2015). https://doi.org/10.1177/0278364914546174

12. Iocchi, L., Nardi, D., Salerno, M.: Reactivity and deliberation: a survey on multi-robot systems. BRSDMAS 2000. LNCS, vol. 2103, pp. 9–32. Springer, Heidelberg (2001). https://doi.org/10.1007/3-540-44568-4_2

13. Konur, S., Dixon, C., Fisher, M.: Formal verification of probabilistic swarm behaviours. In: Dorigo, M., et al. (eds.) ANTS 2010. LNCS, vol. 6234, pp. 440–447. Springer, Heidelberg (2010). https://doi.org/10.1007/978-3-642-15461-4_42

14. Laibinis, L., Pereverzeva, I., Troubitsyna, E.: Formal reasoning about resilient goal-oriented multi-agent systems. Sci. Comput. Program. **148**, 66–87 (2017). https://doi.org/10.1016/j.scico.2017.05.008

15. Laprie, J.: From dependability to resilience. In: 38th IEEE/IFIP International Conference on Dependable Systems and Networks, pp. G8–G9 (2008)

16. Luckcuck, M., Farrell, M., Dennis, L.A., Dixon, C., Fisher, M.: Formal specification and verification of autonomous robotic systems: a survey. CoRR abs/1807.00048 (2018). http://arxiv.org/abs/1807.00048

17. Majd, A., Ashraf, A., Troubitsyna, E., Daneshtalab, M.: Integrating learning, optimization, and prediction for efficient navigation of swarms of drones. In: PDP 2018, pp. 101–108. IEEE Computer Society (2018). https://doi.org/10.1109/PDP2018.2018.00022

18. Majd, A., Troubitsyna, E.: Integrating safety-aware route optimisation and runtime safety monitoring in controlling swarms of drones. In: ISSRE Workshops, pp. 94–95. IEEE Computer Society (2017). https://doi.org/10.1109/ISSREW.2017.63

19. Mitsch, S., Ghorbal, K., Platzer, A.: On provably safe obstacle avoidance for autonomous robotic ground vehicles. In: Robotics: Science and Systems IX (2013). http://www.roboticsproceedings.org/rss09/p14.html

20. Moscato, F., Venticinque, S., Aversa, R., Martino, B.D.: Formal modeling and verification of real-time multi-agent systems: the REMM framework. In: Badica, C., Mangioni, G., Carchiolo, V., Burdescu, D.D. (eds.) IDC 2008. SCI, vol. 162, pp. 187–196. Springer, Heidelberg (2008). https://doi.org/10.1007/978-3-540-85257-5_19
21. Pereverzeva, I.: Formal development of resilient distributed systems. Ph.D. thesis No. 203. Turku Centre for Computer Science (2015). http://urn.fi/URN:ISBN:978-952-12-3253-4
22. Rouff, C.A., Hinchey, M.G., Peña, J., Cortés, A.R.: Using formal methods and agent-oriented software engineering for modeling NASA swarm-based systems. In: 2007 IEEE Swarm Intelligence Symposium, SIS 2007, pp. 348–355. IEEE (2007). https://doi.org/10.1109/SIS.2007.367958
23. Tarasyuk, A., Troubitsyna, E., Laibinis, L.: Integrating stochastic reasoning into Event-B development. Formal Asp. Comput. **27**(1), 53–77 (2015). https://doi.org/10.1007/s00165-014-0305-z
24. Vistbakka, I., Majd, A., Troubitsyna, E.: Deriving mode logic for autonomous resilient systems. In: Sun, J., Sun, M. (eds.) ICFEM 2018. LNCS, vol. 11232, pp. 320–336. Springer, Cham (2018). https://doi.org/10.1007/978-3-030-02450-5_19
25. Vistbakka, I., Majd, A., Troubitsyna, E.: Multi-layered approach to safe navigation of swarms of drones. In: Gallina, B., Skavhaug, A., Schoitsch, E., Bitsch, F. (eds.) SAFECOMP 2018. LNCS, vol. 11094, pp. 112–125. Springer, Cham (2018). https://doi.org/10.1007/978-3-319-99229-7_11
26. Vistbakka, I., Troubitsyna, E., Majd, A.: Multi-layered safety architecture of autonomous systems: formalising coordination perspective. In: HASE 2019, pp. 58–65. IEEE (2019). https://doi.org/10.1109/HASE.2019.00019
27. Webster, M., et al.: Toward reliable autonomous robotic assistants through formal verification: a case study. IEEE Trans. Hum.-Mach. Syst. **46**(2), 186–196 (2016). https://doi.org/10.1109/THMS.2015.2425139
28. Winfield, A.F., Sa, J., Fernandez-Gago, M.C., Dixon, C., Fisher, M.: On formal specification of emergent behaviours in swarm robotic systems. Int. J. Adv. Robot. Syst. **2**(4), 363–370 (2005). https://doi.org/10.5772/5769
29. Zambonelli, F., Jennings, N.R., Wooldridge, M.J.: Developing multiagent systems: the Gaia methodology. ACM Trans. Softw. Eng. Methodol. **12**(3), 317–370 (2003). https://doi.org/10.1145/958961.958963
30. Zhu, X., Liu, Z., Yang, J.: Model of collaborative UAV swarm toward coordination and control mechanisms study. Proc. Comput. Sci. **51**(C), 493–502 (2015). https://doi.org/10.1016/j.procs.2015.05.274

Reactive Middleware for Effective Requirement Change Management of Cloud-Based Global Software Development

David Ebo Adjepon-Yamoah[1,2]([⊠]) (iD)

[1] Ashesi University, 1 University Avenue, Berekuso E/R, PMB 3 CT Cantonment, 00233 Accra, Ghana
`dadjepon@ashesi.edu.gh`
[2] School of Computing, Urban Sciences Building, Science Central, Newcastle-upon-Tyne NE4 5TG, UK
`d.e.adjepon-yamoah@ncl.ac.uk`

Abstract. Requirement change management (RCM) for global software development (GSD), facilitated by the cloud platform, faces communication, coordination and control issues especially when there is no effective information and knowledge-sharing mechanisms. This paper describes a reasonably effective requirement change management approach for cloud-based GSD.

Objective: In this regard, we contribute a Reactive Middleware which facilitates a set of guidelines defined to manage change and traceability.

Methods: This Reactive Middleware provides services for user management, requirement management, change management, and traceability of cloud-based GSD projects. We present (1) a process model for change management and traceability (CM-T) for cloud-based GSD, and then (2) detail our management approach for system engineering processes as part of the presented GSD guidelines.

Results: To ensure that the defined CM-T process model complies with the CMMI Level 2 (Baseline) Capability, the process model is validated using an expert panel review process where a total average, *85.58%* of the experts support the maturity of the process model. Also, we demonstrate the continual tight linkage of stakeholders' requirements and system engineering processes towards change management and traceability, with an Airlock Control System case study.

Keywords: Requirements change management · Traceability · CMMI Level 2 · Global software development · Cloud computing

1 Introduction

Many software development projects are globally distributed in nature [18], resulting in the evolution of the term Global Software Development (GSD)

© Springer Nature Switzerland AG 2019
R. Calinescu and F. Di Giandomenico (Eds.): SERENE 2019, LNCS 11732, pp. 46–66, 2019.
https://doi.org/10.1007/978-3-030-30856-8_4

[3,10]. It is for this reason why cloud computing is well fit as a facilitating delivery model for GSD [8]. This model enables ubiquitous, convenient, on-demand network access to a shared pool of configurable computing resources (e.g., networks, services, storages, applications, and services) that can be rapidly provisioned and released with minimal management effort or service provider interaction [16]. GSD seems to have become a business necessity for various reasons, including cost, scarcity of resources, and the need to locate development closer to customers [9]. Fundamentally, GSD involves communication for information exchange, coordination of teams, activities and artefacts so they contribute to the overall objective, and the control of teams [8].

Communication, coordination and control issues arise largely when there is no effective information and knowledge-sharing mechanisms [5]. In GSD, due to lack of common understanding between geographically dispersed teams, requirements management is particularly difficult [14]. Here, changes to requirements that are inadequately managed affect product quality [13]. Hence, the requirement change management plays a vital part of software requirements engineering process in GSD. However, the communication issue and requirement change management in GSD are given very little consideration as compared to localised software development [6,12]. In order to make any meaningful headway for GSD, the concepts of requirements change management, and traceability of these requirements through the development life-cycle in the context of the distributed development resources, need to be appropriately considered. Our research contributes a Reactive Middleware that manages change and traceability for cloud-based GSD. This contribution satisfies four objectives: (*O1*) - define a change management and treaceabily (CM-T) process model, which applies a software process improvement method to ensure the maturity of the requirement change management (RCM) and traceability processes, (*O2*) - identify a standard quality management framework to facilitate a significant level of quality for the proposed CM-T process model, (*O3*) - validate the CM-T process model using an expert panel review process, and (*O4*) - demonstrate the defined management guidelines by applying it to an Airlock Control System case study.

2 Related Work

Two similar works (i.e. [4] and [5]) representing the identified discourse of the state-of-the-art are described briefly. In [4], the authors present a method consisting of three stages: (i) an understanding of the changes required between different GSD sites is to be established; (ii) a change analysis is to be performed with respect to the development work, which might be either directly or indirectly affected by the changes; and (iii) a finalization of the changes will be made between GSD sites. They validate their method by applying it to a case study of an online shopping system, where the roles of stakeholders were played by a group of students. The limitation is largely in terms of the lack of rigour in the validation process, as it is not validated by experts. Also, [5] aims to provide a framework to manage RCM using Cased-Based Reasoning technique (CBR).

Table 1. Mapping the steps for effective requirements management & traceability processes with proposed change management & traceability services

5 key steps	Proposed change management and traceability services
Trace creation and maintenance	The PSS facilitates the initiation of change requests and receiving change notifications
Detect change	The AMS monitors the relevant artefacts for changes, and then triggers the PSS to notify appropriate stakeholders or change agents
Analyse change impact	The GSD Team Members manage the development process and change with its impact using the GSD guidelines
Check for consistency	When there are change requests that are related to the high priority requirements, the GSD change managers apply the change management and traceability process (CM-T) model to approve, note or disapprove the request
Propagate change	This CM-T model takes into consideration the bidirectional traceability of the change agents (i.e. system stakeholders, artefacts and tools) involved in the change request

CBR is used to effect change in requirements based on previous knowledge and experience. This work defines a form of artificial intelligence to manage requirement changes. Their proposed framework is evaluated using an experimental study.

3   Reactive Middleware

Our position paper [2], introduces the Reactive Middleware (RM), which is a critical component of the Reactive Architecture [1]. It is composed of the Publish/Subscribe system(PSS) and the Artefacts Monitoring system (AMS). The RM interacts with system stakeholders, and other components of the Reactive Architecture (i.e. System Engineering Tools, and a Shared Artefacts Repository). The RM facilitates management guidelines for GSD projects that applies quality process management, to a change management and traceability process model. In Table 1, we provide a mapping of a literature-based focus of five key steps for effective requirements management and traceability processes to our proposed approach facilitated as services by the Reactive Middleware.

3.1   Publish/Subscribe System

This system implements a Publish/Subscribe mechanism. Here, all actors (i.e. system stakeholders and tools) involved in the development and evolution of an artefact subscribe to that artefact (see Table 7). Artefacts can only be accessed by specific authorised actors. The PSS identifies "change" and notifies all the actors that have registered their interest in the artefact. That said, the Publish/Subscribe System specifically provides services for user management as the stakeholders register to use the Reactive Middleware, and roles and privileges are assigned to them. Also, the system provides services for requirements management.

3.2 Artefacts Monitoring/Interpretation System

The AMS interacts with the Shared Artefacts Repository to monitor changes made to artefacts. The Open Services for Lifecycle Collaboration (OSLC) technology [15] used for *monitoring* in AMS provides standardised methods to represent, access, and link to resources. With OSLC specifications, tools can freely understand each other's data and artefacts. This makes it easy to better analyse, track, and explore that data to make better decisions. There are features to support change management, traceability, etc. Projects and their composing elements being developed in development environments are tagged with OSLC annotations, to reveal their artefacts (see Table 7) to client plug-ins.

3.3 Management Guidelines for System Engineering

We introduce the defined management guidelines for GSDs (see Table 8). The GSD guideline defines a generic development policy for software engineering projects. As part of the GSD guidelines, we present our derivative of PMBOK [17] process group for managing quality system engineering processes, and then a CM-T process model. The PMBOK process group for managing quality system processes (see Fig. 6), plays an overarching role in the GSD guidelines. This management approach is applied to the CM-T process model.

PMBOK 5-Step Process Group for System Engineering Life-Cycle. The PMBOK is a project management guide that is a well accepted standard which provides a general framework for project management. The PMBOK contains 42 project management (PM) practices organised by two orthogonal categories: *Process Groups* (PG) and *Knowledge Areas* (KA). Here, each of the 42 processes belongs to exactly one process group and to exactly one knowledge area. The PG organisation shows the project's life cycle (see Fig. 6), involving 5 groups: Initiating, Planning, Executing, Monitoring & Control, and Closing.

Change Management and Traceability Process Model. The CM-T process model is expected to ensure a *matured* change management and traceability processes relative to the specific practices of the CMMI Level 2 [7]. To begin the definition of the process model, we indicate the main processes involved in validating the CM-T process model as to:

A. Provide objective(s) for building the model
We aim to develop a model that represents key practices in RE within a maturity framework (see Fig. 7). Here, our objectives are:

- A primary objective of our CM-T model is to guide software stakeholders to relate key change management and traceability processes to goals in order to prioritise their requirements process improvement activities.
- The CM-T process model should strengthen components of the CMMI (involving software requirements) to clearly focus on the change management and traceability processes.
- Our model should complement the CMMI (Level 2) so that practitioners are not required to learn another software process improvement methodology.
- Finally, we aim to link theory to practice through a model that is easy to use and interpret.

B. Show the criteria identified during the initial stages of model development

We initially identify six relevant success criteria based on CMMI Level 2 baseline capability (see Fig. 7) to guide the development of the CM-T model. Success criteria were established per evaluation question. These success criteria are presented in Table 2. The criteria were identified using a method similar to that used in the SPICE trials to support the ISO/IEC 15504 emerging standard. The resulting CM-T process model (see Fig. 8) considers the development teams and system engineering tools as the main *agents of change*. From the point where an accepted change is being effected till the point where it has been implemented successfully, a process to trace all the change with regards to participating stakeholders, associated software development life-cycle (SDLC) phase, corresponding system engineering tools, impact on other artefacts, etc. is undertaken in parallel. This period also sees the creation or modifications to system documentations. At this point, the *change managers* accept the change and it is marked as successful. Then a generation of notification to all stakeholders of the change, and finally the change request is closed.

C. Design a validation instrument to test the success criteria (to include methods for reporting/analysing responses)

We design a validation instrument to test the success criteria provided in Fig. 7. We choose a questionnaire as a validation instrument since it mainly provide relatively precise responses for evaluations,compared with interviews. We consider a set of experts who provides their responses to the questionnaire for validation (Table 4).

The validation process meeting objective (i.e. **D. Select an expert panel to reflect the population of experts in Software Engineering, Requirements Engineering (RE), and CMMI**), and the reporting process meeting objective (i.e. **E. Present results of the validation instrument**) are presented as the validation of the CM-T process model by the expert panel and evaluation of Reactive Middleware with regards to the services it provides respectively in Sect. 4.

Table 2. CM-T process model validation

Criterion	Purpose	Rule	Source
Adherence to CMM characteristics	The new model should be recognisable as a derivative of established models - both in structure and concept. By tapping into the established models, the CM-T model takes the strengths of a proven improvement structures and becomes more accessible and compatible, avoiding redundant activities	- CMM maturity level concepts must be implemented - Each level should have a theme consistent with CMM - Requirement engineering (RE) processes must be integrated - The model should be recognisable as a CMM offshoot - The CM-T must be systematic and sequential	Where possible we should adapt existing models rather than create new ones Maturity levels help characterise a process and set out a strategy for its improvement
Limit scope	CMM goals, RE phases and RE processes define the boundaries of the model. The model does not include all RE processes	- Key activities relating to technical and organisational RE processes are included - Processes are prioritised - Processes relate directly to the CM-T process areas - The scope/level of detail should be appropriate (i.e. depth and breadth of processes presented)	It is important to know the scope of the model, i.e. what the model includes and excludes
Consistency	Having an acceptable level of 'construct' validity will help users navigate within levels of maturity as well as between different levels of process maturity. Model development and adaptation depends on an acceptable level of consistency	- There should be consistent use of terms and CMM features at this level of development - There will be a consistency in structure between model components at the same level of granularity that are modelling different maturity levels	To understand a model it is important that there is a common language. Each stage of development should describe processes at similar levels of granularity
Understandable	All users of the model should have a shared understanding of the RE process in order to identify where improvement is needed. There should be no ambiguity in interpretation, especially when goals are set for improvement	- All terms should be clearly defined (i.e. have only one meaning) - All relationships between processes and model architecture should be unambiguous and functional	The importance of clear definitions. Understanding is a prerequisite for effective process improvement and management
Ease of use	Over-complex models are unlikely to be adopted as they require extra resources and may be too challenging for the user to interpret without extensive training. The model will have differing levels of decomposition starting with the most high level in order to gradually lead the user through from a descriptive model towards a more prescriptive solution	- The model should be decomposed to a level that is simple to understand - The model should be simple yet retain meaning - The chunks of information should clearly relate as they develop into more complex structures - The model should require little or no training to be used	Usability is a key requirement of any process improvement model
Verifiable	Model strengths and weaknesses need to be tested to help direct future model development. Validation of the model will help to improve the model, add confidence in its representation and help with research in this area	- The model must be verifiable, i.e. we must be able to test/measure how well model meet its objectives and whether meeting these objectives leads to a high quality CM-T process model	To assess whether a process is useful, well implemented the model needs to be verifiable

Table 3. Meeting the high level requirements of an effective GSD framework

GSD requirements	Description of approaches
Effective information and knowledge sharing:	
R1: Artefact independence	Artefacts in the Shared Artefacts Repository are saved in their original formats, some generic XML derivatives are generated for interoperability, as well as the generation of metadata for each artefact in XML format to facilitate change management and traceability. (**GS6**)
R2: Supports globally distributed development	The Reactive Middleware is deployed to the cloud environment to facilitate global accessibility. Also, it provides GSD services towards user management, requirement management, change management, and traceability. (**GS1, GS2, GS3, GS4, GS5, GS7**)
R3: Ability to handle different and large numbers of changing artefacts	The Shared Artefacts Repository has a high scalable capacity for varying formats of artefacts. Also, the CM-T process model has been designed to keep up with large volumes of changing to artefacts. An Airlock Control System case study has been provided in Sect. 4.2 to assess this. (**GS9, GS10,** and **GS11**)
Automation:	
R4: Automated as far as possible	The Reactive Middleware has been developed as a set of cloud-based REST web services to provide the mentioned set of GSD services. It mainly minimizes the manual effort involved in artefact consistency management involving change management and traceability. (**GS8, GS11, GS12,** and **GS13**)
Diversity of tools:	
R5: Tool integration	The System Engineering Toolbox provides a set of tools with different versions. These tools are integrated using the OSLC technology such that a workflow can be created. Also, outputs of one tool is reformated as an input for another. Plug-in for the toolbox is provided for variations of the Eclipse development environment. (**GS5**)

4   Reactive Middleware Evaluation

First, we validate the CM-T process model by conducting an "expert panel review process". This is used to assess the maturity of the CM-T process model in light of the CMMI Level 2 specific practices - requirements change management. Secondly, we demonstrate the continuous tight linkage between requirements and system engineering processes provided by the introduced GSD guidelines, by an Airlock Control System case study. At this point, we present our research question as "How

Table 4. Constitution of the expert panel

Name of participant	Current institution	Position/relevant experience
1. M. Mehr (Ph.D.)	School of Computer Science, Newcastle University, UK	Researcher (expert in RE methods and Security)
2. S. Alajrami (Ph.D.)	Praqma, Norway	DevOps Consultant, and trained SPICE Assessor
3. R. Ebrahimy (Ph.D.)	DTU, Denmark	Post-Doc (expert in RE methods)
4. D. M. Dias (Ph.D.)	KernKonzept, Germany	Systems Verification Engineer and Programmer
5. R. Materre (Ph.D.)	School of Computer Science, Newcastle University, UK	Post-Doc (expert in RE methods)
6. S. F. Shahandashti (Ph.D.)	Department of Computer Science, University of York, UK	Lecturer (expert in RE methods and Security)
7. L. L. Bastos	Accenture, Newcastle, UK	Software Engineer and trained ISO 9001 Auditor
8. P. B. Mahama	Blue Oak System Ltd., Ghana	Quality Manager, IT Business Analyst - requirements, and Programmer
9. E. Dadzie	IT Systems Quality Control, United States Department of Agriculture, USA	Quality Manager and SPICE Assessor
10. E. Toreini (Ph.D.)	School of Computer Science, Newcastle University, UK	Post-Doc (expert in RE methods)
11. R. Ahmed	Department of Computer Science, Sulaimani Polytechnic University, Iraq	Lecturer (expert in RE methods and Security)
12. Z. Wen (Ph.D.)	School of Computer Science, Newcastle University, UK	Post-Doc (expert in RE methods)
13. M. Dzandu	School of Computer Science, University of Reading, UK	Ph.D. Student and Lecturer (expert in RE methods)
14. Anonymous	TalkTalk, UK	SCRUM Master and Quality Manager
15. Anonymous	School of Computer Science, Tallinn University, Estonia	Senior Lecturer (expert in RE methods)
16. Anonymous	Institute for Applied Software Systems Engineering, Clausthal University of Technology, Germany	Senior Research Associate (expert in RE methods)

can the Reactive Middleware guide system engineering to ensure the continual tight linkage of stakeholders' requirements and system engineering processes?".

4.1   Analysis of Expert Review

At this stage, we evaluate whether the motivation for building the Reactive Middlware's CM-T process model is justified, and if the process model is matured in relation to the CMMI Level 2 practice for managing change and traceability. We consider the use of expert panels to validate a software process model, and the constitution of this panel is presented in Table 4. Then, we present our analysis of the feedback from the experts on the maturity of the CM-T model processes in light of the CMMI Level 2 (baseline) capability. In this expert review, a panel of sixteen experts are constituted to validate the change management and traceability (CM-T) process model. Here, seven experts are from the industry, while nine are from academia. Experts from the industry are selected based on their experience in requirements engineering (RE) and software process improvement (SPI). Also, the research focus (i.e. RE and SPI) and publications of academics informed their selection. To facilitate the collection of data from the panel, a designed questionnaire is used as our data collection method. We classify the questionnaire in relevant sections covering the "assessment of expertise" and the six relevant success criteria for validating the CM-T model. The responses from the experts are expected to be classified as "Strongly agree", "Agree", "Neutral", "Disagree", "Strongly disagree". The "Neutral" option caters for both "uncertainty" and "no opinion" or "unwillingness to answer".

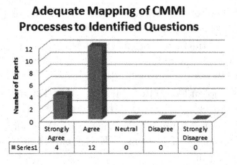

Fig. 1. Adherence to CMMI characteristics: the CMMI processes have been adequately mapped to the identified questions?

Considering Success Criteria One - "Adherence to CMMI Characteristics" - (see Fig. 1), all the sixteen (16) experts agree that the CMMI processes have been adequately mapped to the identified questions. Here, four (4) experts "strongly agree", and twelve (12) "agree".

In the assessment of the expertise of the panel, we identified that 100% of the experts indicated their expertise in both "Software" or "System Engineering", "RE" and in "SPI". However out of the sixteen experts, one indicated no

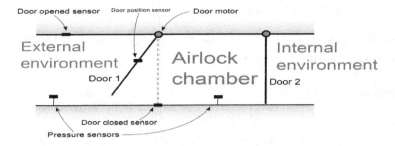

Fig. 2. The airlock control system

expertise in "CMMI". In terms of validating the CM-T model, a total average of *84.38%* of the experts at least agree (i.e. indicating "Strongly agree" and "Agree") to the six (6) success criteria of the CM-T model. This high percentage of acceptance indicates the high level of conformance of the CM-T model to the CMMI Level 2 baseline processes. The composition of this high percentage is that, an average of *60.94%* of the experts "strongly agree", and also an average of *23.44%* of the experts "agree" to the questions in the questionnaire relating to the success criteria of the CM-T model. That said, *100%* of the experts "disagree" that "a considerable amount of prior knowledge of CMMI is needed to be able to interpret the CM-T model" under the "ease of use" success criteria. With this supportive choice, a new total average of *85.58%* of the experts accept the maturity of the CM-T model. It must also be mentioned that an average of *14.42%* chose to remain "neutral" on the questions. For those who remained "neutral", we gathered three general comments from them, that we will consider in future work:

1. Ambiguous process definitions for the "Consistency" criteria.
2. The CM-T process model is incomplete for the "Adherence to CMMI Characteristics" criteria.
3. The assessment component is not self-explanatory for the "Verification" criteria.

4.2   Airlock Control System Case Study

An airlock control system (ACS) (see Fig. 2) case study from [11] is used to demonstrate the proposed management guidelines provided by the Reactive Middleware. The main function of the ACS is to separate two areas (i.e. external and internal) with different air pressures and allow users to pass safely between the areas. Let us assume that the pressure outside is lower than inside. The system is equipped with a number of actuators - door motors, a pressure pump, as well as sensors - pressure sensors, door positions sensors and buttons. The goal of the GSD Team members spread over three geographical areas (i.e. Europe, Africa and Australia), is to develop control software that would allow a user to safely

Table 5. Classified requirements of the airlock control system

*Airlock Control System Requirements (Resilient Quality Attribute - **SAFETY**)*		
Requirements classification	ID	Requirements
Environment	ENV1	The airlock system separates two different environments. The pressure of the external environment is lower than that of the internal one
	ENV2	In order to maintain different pressures, the two environments must be physically separated
	ENV3	The system has two doors and a chamber. Each door when closed separates the chamber from the appropriate environment
	ENV4	Each door is equipped with three positioning sensors and a two-way motor. The sensors consist of two boolean sensors representing the fully closed (*SNS_CLOSED*) and opened (*SNS_OPENED*) door states, and a range-value position sensor (*SNS_POS*) that returns values in a range between the fully closed and the fully opened states inclusively. The two-way motor (*ACT_MOTOR*) is the actuator that can open and close the door within its physical range of movement
	ENV5	There is a pressure sensor in each of the areas, three in total (*SNS_PRESSURE_OUT*, *SNS_PRESSURE_CHAMBER, SNS_PRESSURE_IN*)
	ENV6	The pressure in the chamber can be changed by the pump actuator (*ACT_PUMP*)
	ENV7	Any of the sensors and actuators may fail to provide a correct function
Safety	SAF1	The pressure in the chamber must always be between the lower external pressure and the higher internal one
	SAF2	A door can only be opened if the pressure values in the chamber and the conjoined environment are equal
	SAF3	Only one door is allowed to be opened at any moment of time
	SAF4	The pressure in the chamber shall not be changed unless both doors are closed
Function	FUN1	When in operation, the airlock system must be able to let users pass safely between the two environments via the airlock

pass through the airlock. The GSD teams at Europe, Africa and Asia prioritise the safety properties (i.e. SAF1, SAF2, SAF3 and SAF4) of the ACS, leaving aside issues of its usability, operation speed, reliability and maintainability. It must be mentioned that safety properties described in this section do not completely cover all safety concerns that would arise for a real system. We only focus on a part of system properties described in this section to limit the context of the case study. The high-level requirements of the system are presented in Table 5.

Table 6. Classified steps of GSD guidelines

Classification of the steps of GSD guidelines into services	
Services	GSD Guidelines Steps ID
User management	GS1 and GS2
Requirement management	GS3 and GS4
Change management	GS5, GS6, GS7, GS8, GS10, GS11, and GS12
Traceability	GS9 and GS13

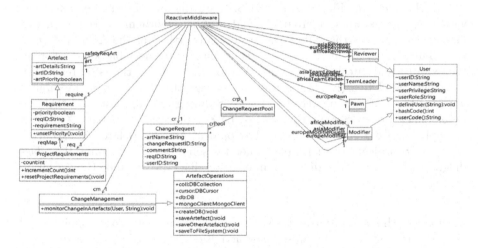

Fig. 3. Class diagram of the airlock control system case study

GSD Guidelines for ACS Development. The ACS case study is used as a running example of the Reactive Middleware's GSD guidelines. We implement a prototype of the Reactive Middleware and use it to demonstrate its set of services (see Fig. 3). Here, the development of Company X's (i.e. an assumed owning company name with simulated developers) ACS case study is guided by this set of guidelines. These guidelines can be classified with respect to the Reactive Middleware's services (see Table 6). However, the ACS case study presents the above classification under the five basic "process groups" (PG) (refer to Fig. 6) of the PMBOK specific "knowledge area" (KA) of "project quality management". Company X expects that an effective change management and traceability in the development process of the ACS will improve the quality of the management of the project.

Initiating the ACS Project. The ACS is the core product of Company X. Company X sends some of its development activities offshore, but maintains a team of practitioners (i.e. Team Europe) in the European based central office who work mainly from 9 am to 5 pm five days a week. This team focuses on requirements gathering, prioritising requirements (and focus on "safety-related requirements"), developing their core product, managing the offshore or GSD teams, and testing the bespoke software. The other GSD teams are more focused on product deployment and integration. This approach ensures a continuous and around the clock development of the ACS. As part of Company X's ACS development policy, the Reactive Middleware is used to aid the effective management of the project, as well as to provide an automated facility to ensure that a matured (i.e. CMMI-compliant) change management and traceability process model is applied.

Planning the ACS Project. Team Europe focuses on the development of the airlock chamber (see Fig. 2) of the ACS. Since the airlock chamber interfaces with both the external environment and internal environment, the team can manage the changes that affect the "safety properties" of the ACS, and their traceability. Also, Team Africa and Team Asia are responsible for developing the external and internal environments respectively. Here, the GSD teams use the cloud-based Reactive Middleware to manage the changes and traceability affecting the "safety properties" of the ACS during development, and that the development processes meet the "CMMI Level 2 practice". Company X decides to apply the GSD guidelines to its development process. Before the execution of the ACS project, Team Europe generates some project diagrams (i.e. class diagram - Fig. 3, package diagram, interaction diagram) to guide the execution process.

Executing the ACS Project. At this point, team leaders are appointed for the three respective GSD teams. These activities are guided by the **user management** set of guidelines (i.e. **GS1** and **GS2**). Here, team leaders play the role of "Team Leader" with an associated privilege of "Own" where they have permission to perform any activities on development artefacts. Also, team leaders assign roles (e.g. "Reviewer", "Modifier", "Pawn", etc.) and privileges (i.e. "Review", "Modify", "View" respectively) to team members. Then the team leaders form the development supervisory team referred to as the "GSD Change Managers". This GSD Change Managers perform a crucial role of managing changes that affects prioritised ACS "safety requirements", and "trace" the changes' cause-and-effect on requirements and associated artefacts. The next set of activities relating to the ACS requirements are guided by the **requirements management** set of guidelines (i.e. **GS3** and **GS4**). Firstly, the ACS requirements are assigned as either a priority or not, and then they are uniquely identified. The GSD Change Managers set the safety requirements as the priority for this project. After all these activities have been undertaken, the three GSD teams begin the development of the ACS. Here, the development of the three ACS environments are developed as well as the doors, sensors and actuators.

Monitoring and Controlling the ACS Project. The GSD Change Managers together with some project stakeholders at the central office in Europe, "monitor and control" the development process to meet the project requirements (i.e. safety). In this activity, a set of the GSD guidelines are for **change management** (i.e. **GS5**, **GS6**, **GS7**, **GS8**, **GS10**, **GS11**, and **GS12**) and **traceability** (i.e. **GS9** and **GS13**).

```
**************************
CHANGE MANAGEMENT - CM
**************************

Creating CHANGE REQUESTS...

*CHANGE REQUEST POOL:

Change Request: [CR1685232414]:
(ActionPPMachine.class, ROO3, SAF3, 'Prioritising the opening of door
requests from both the internal or external environments')

Change Request: [CR280744458]:
(artName1, ROO3, ENV3, 'Colour of door is critical to safety')

*Is Priority of Requirement (SAF3) HIGH?: [true]

*[Sign-Off CHANGE REQUEST]: 'approve', 'note' OR 'disapprove':-

Decision: [approve]

Change Request Details:
Change Request: [CR1685232414]:
(ActionPPMachine.class, ROO3, SAF3, 'Prioritising the opening of door
requests from both the internal or external environments')

Change Request decision is [approve]
```

Fig. 4. Snippet of the terminal output for the reactive middleware change management service for the airlock control system case study

During the development process, a set of "change requests" relative to the ACS requirements are raised. This process requires the CM-T process model of the Reactive Middleware. The steps of the CM-T process model are followed to resolve all "change requests". Change requests are expected to contain information about the artefact involved, the identification of the initiating stakeholder, the relevant requirement identification, and the change request details. Here, two change requests are submitted to the change request pool (see Fig. 4). The GSD Change Managers consider the change requests based on their priority, and then select which one to make a decision on. At this point, GSD Change Managers decide that the change request with identification *CR1685232414* is of high priority (SAF3) and needs to be considered first.

The team leader for Team Asia that presented the change request defends the criticality of the request, and leads the decision-making process. As a result of the need for such a change, the change request is *approved* by the GSD Change

```
*******************************
TRACE ARTEFACT CHANGE - Trace
*******************************

[Trace] Trigger Change in artefact by [R003]:- Feng Jiabao

[CHANGE MANAGEMENT -CM] process(es)...
[CM- SAME FILENAMES] Retrieved Artefact Name: 'e:\ActionPPMachine.class'
[CM- SAME HASH] Hash of Input Artefact [-614419020], and Hash of Ouput
Artefact [-614419020] ---> ChunkSize: 261120

[TRACEABILITY -trace] process(es)...

[Trace Changed Artefact [e:\ActionPPMachine.class] --> '2016/11/19 00:03:49'
begins...]
             [Trace --> UserID]: R003,
             [Trace --> Artefact]: e:\ActionPPMachine.class,
             [Trace --> Notification]: [CM- TRIGGER] Change Request on:
*'e:\ActionPPMachine.class' by User[R003]

[Trace --> Changed Artefact [e:\ActionPPMachine.class] -->2016/11/19 00:03:49
ends]

[CM- TRIGGER] Change Request on: *'e:\ActionPPMachine.class' by User[R003]

[Trace Summary]
****************

[Trace]:---> CHANGED ARTEFACT:
Artefacts Details: [ART2537339]:- 'Only one <door> is allowed to be <opened>
at any moment of <time>.'

[Trace]:---> CHANGED AGENT: (R003) - Feng Jiabao

[Trace]:---> CAUSE-AND-EFFECT on ARTEFACTS:
(1)Artefacts Details: [ART2537337]:- 'The <pressure> in the <chamber> must
always be between the <lower external pressure> and the <higher internal
pressure>.'

(2)Artefacts Details: [ART2537338]:- 'A <door> can only be <opened> if the
<pressure values> in the <chamber> and the conjoined <environment> are
equal.'

(3)Artefacts Details: [ART2537340]:- 'The <pressure> in the <chamber> shall
not be changed unless both <doors> are <closed>.'

Sent message: '[CM- TRIGGER] Change Request on: *'e:\ActionPPMachine.class'
by User[R003] : Thread-1 : 972210874' :--> 1659654801 : Thread-1

Received: '[CM- TRIGGER] Change Request on: *'e:\ActionPPMachine.class' by
User[R003] : Thread-1 : 972210874'

Notification: [Key: 1498854882]--> Value: '[CM- TRIGGER] Change Request on:
*'e:\ActionPPMachine.class' by User[R003] : Thread-1 : 972210874'
```

Fig. 5. Snippet of the terminal output for the reactive middleware traceability service for the airlock control system case study

Managers. The decision taken for *CR1685232414* is logged as part of the documentation of the change request. The initiator (i.e. *R003*) of the change request is notified to "effect the change". Effecting this change requires a close monitoring by the team leader of Team Asia to make sure that it is undertaken as expected. The team leader assesses the process, and then "verifies and validates" the change. The next step involves a detailed assessment of the "cause-and-effect" of the change on project artefacts, and all minor conflicts are resolved within the local GSD team. A process to "trace" the change with regards to participating stakeholders, associated software processes, system engineering tools, impact on other artefacts, etc. is undertaken in parallel with development (see Fig. 5). The activities for tracing changes also facilitates "roll-back" of actions. This activity is guided by the set of GSD guidelines (i.e. GS9 and GS13). Finally, the GSD Change Managers accept the change and the change process is marked as successful. All relevant stakeholders in Team Asia are sent a notification of the change. The change request is then "closed".

Closing the ACS Project. Here, the system is demonstrated to the project stakeholders (i.e. Project Approval Board of Company X, relevant users). The stakeholders qualitatively evaluate the ACS according to the prioritised requirements and expectations. In this process, highlights of the ACS development process are identified, discussed, and lessons learnt.

5 Threats to Validity

5.1 Ensuring Traceability

The CM-T process model is facilitated in terms of change management and traceability by the OSLC approach. Here, the limitation of this process model is that the correctness of each consistency management stage is heavily reliant upon the correctness of trace links. OSLC is very effective in identifying artefacts and resources within artefacts. The dependence on trace links between artefacts raises the question of how CM-T process model could be more tolerant to errors introduced during trace creation, especially for a GSD service (i.e. CM-TaaS) based on the rapidly evolving cloud platform. This is a significant issue considering that the current approach to creating trace links using the OSLC, by nature, is not likely to provide 100% accuracy. Thus, user intervention is required to ensure correct links are established prior to consistency management.

5.2 Constitution of the Expert Panel

The constitution of the expert panel is from colleagues at Newcastle University, researchers and practitioners from conferences attended, and other experts who were identified through their research or industrial work. These experts were selected exclusively based on their expertise. That said, the varying levels of the relationship between some of the experts and the author could be perceived as a source of bias. Despite some polarisation of views, there was relatively strong agreement that the requirement engineering process is in need of further support and hence, the CM-T process model has a high potential of enhancing this process.

6 Conclusion

We mainly contribute a Reactive Middleware that applies our defined CM-T process model (see objective *O1*), within the context of an adapted PMBOK quality process management approach to cloud-based GSD (see objective *O2*). The Reactive Middleware provides services for user management, requirement management, change management and traceability, and are facilitated by our GSD management guidelines. To ensure that the defined CM-T process model complies with the CMMI Level 2 (Baseline) Capability, the CM-T process model is validated using an expert panel review process where a total average *85.58%* of the experts supported the maturity of the CM-T process model (see objective

O3). Also, we demonstrate the application of the GSD management guidelines provided by the Reactive Middleware with an Airlock Control System case study (see objective *O4*). By this, we highlight the continual tight linkage of stakeholders' requirements and system engineering processes towards change management and traceability.

Appendix

Table 7. Description of artefacts in the shared artefacts repository

SDLC phases	Artefacts description
Requirements	System requirements documents are obtained from tools such as ProR
Specification	System model specifications as artefacts contain elements such as invariants, guards, actions, etc. Such elements are also extracted as dependent artefacts
Implementation	Implementable source codes of model specifications are generated with appropriate tools such as EB2ALL. It supports automatic code generation from Event-B to C, C++, Java and C#. Another tool example is EventB2Dafny. This tool extends the Boogie and Dafny tools, and allows the use of Dafny static analysis machinery based on design-by-contract principles. This yields artefacts in the form of executable input code for Boogie and Dafny tools
Documentation	Documentation artefacts are in the form of: (1) traceability logs, (2) incident reports, and (3) others such as designs, test plans, execution results, etc.

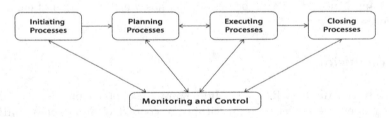

Fig. 6. PMBOK® process group for system engineering life-cycle

Table 8. Global software development management guidelines

Guidelines steps ID	Guidelines
GS1	System development teams should appoint team leaders
GS2	These team leaders will constitute the GSD change managers
GS3	System requirements should be classified based on identified dependability quality attributes (i.e. safety, reliability, robustness, etc.), and are then prioritised relative to their importance to the system stakeholders
GS4	Team leaders must assign roles to all team members with the prioritised requirements in mind, and manage the development process with the adapted PMBOK guide
GS5	All other change agents especially the system engineering tools should be assigned a default privilege of review
GS6	All system artefacts should be saved in a shared artefacts repository
GS7	The privileges (i.e. none, view, modify, review, own) of system stakeholders or change agents will determine the access privileges to system artefacts
GS8	Change agents must subscribe to relevant artefacts after they are created, in order to receive notifications when they are changed
GS9	All related artefacts must be linked together to facilitate traceability
GS10	Changes made to any system artefacts must be logged
GS11	When changes affect the high priority set of requirements, appropriate local team leader must lead the change request review process (i.e. involving the CM-T model) of the GSD change managers
GS12	On the other hand, conflicts arising from changes to low priority set of requirements are resolved locally, lead by the local team leader
GS13	Changes in system artefacts should be traceable to manage its impact on related/linked requirements or artefacts

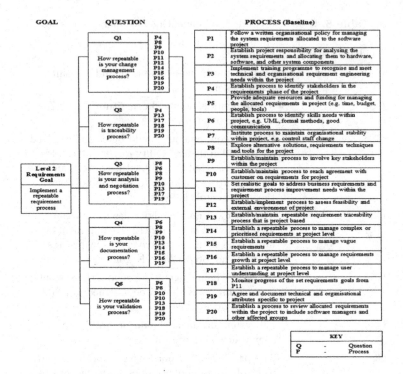

GOAL	QUESTION		PROCESS (Baseline)	
	Q1	P4 P6 P9 P10 P11 P12 P14 P15 P16 P19 P20	P1	Follow a written organisational policy for managing the system requirements allocated to the software project
	How repeatable is your change management process?		P2	Establish project responsibility for analysing the system requirements and allocating them to hardware, software, and other system components
			P3	Implement training programme to recognise and meet technical and organisational requirement engineering needs within the project
	Q2	P4 P13 P17 P18 P19 P20	P4	Establish process to identify stakeholders in the requirements phase of the project
	How repeatable is traceability process?		P5	Provide adequate resources and funding for managing the allocated requirements in project (e.g. time, budget, people, tools)
			P6	Establish process to identify skills needs within project, e.g. UML, formal methods, good communication
			P7	Institute process to maintain organisational stability within project, e.g. control staff change
Level 2 Requirements Goal	Q3	P5 P6 P8 P9 P10 P13 P17 P19	P8	Explore alternative solutions, requirements techniques and tools for the project
Implement a repeatable requirement process	How repeatable is your analysis and negotiation process?		P9	Establish/maintain process to involve key stakeholders within the project
			P10	Establish/maintain process to reach agreement with customer on requirements for project
			P11	Set realistic goals to address business requirements and requirement process improvement needs within the project
	Q4	P6 P8 P9 P10 P13 P14 P16 P19	P12	Establish/implement process to assess feasibility and external environment of project
	How repeatable is your documentation process?		P13	Establish/maintain repeatable requirement traceability process that is project based
			P14	Establish a repeatable process to manage complex or prioritised requirements at project level
			P15	Establish a repeatable process to manage vague requirements
			P16	Establish a repeatable process to manage requirements growth at project level
	Q5	P6 P8 P10 P10 P13 P18 P19 P20	P17	Establish a repeatable process to manage user understanding at project level
	How repeatable is your validation process?		P18	Monitor progress of the set requirements goals from P11
			P19	Agree and document technical and organisational attributes specific to project
			P20	Establish a process to review allocated requirements within the project to include software managers and other affected groups

	KEY	
Q	-	Question
P	-	Process

Fig. 7. Candidate processes reflecting a CMMI level 2 (baseline) capability

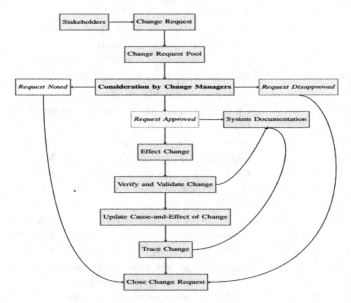

Fig. 8. Change management and traceability process model

References

1. Adjepon-Yamoah, D., Romanovsky, A., Iliasov, A.: A reactive architecture for cloud-based system engineering. In: Proceedings of the 2015 International Conference on Software and System Process, ICSSP 2015, pp. 77–81. ACM, New York (2015). https://doi.org/10.1145/2785592.2785611
2. Adjepon-Yamoah, D.E.: Towards dependable change management and traceability for global software development. arXiv preprint arXiv:1608.05981 (2016)
3. Akbar, M.A., et al.: Success factors influencing requirements change management process in global software development. J. Comput. Lang. **51**, 112–130 (2019). https://doi.org/10.1016/j.cola.2018.12.005.   http://www.sciencedirect.com/scien ce/article/pii/S1045926X18301411
4. Ali, N., Lai, R.: A method of requirements change management for global software development. Inf. Softw. Technol. **70**, 49–67 (2016). https://doi.org/10.1016/j. infsof.2015.09.005. http://www.sciencedirect.com/science/article/pii/S095058491 5001640
5. Ali, S., Iqbal, N., Hafeez, Y.: Towards requirement change management for global software development using case base reasoning. Mehran Univ. Res. J. Eng. Technol. **37**(3), 639–652 (2018). https://doi.org/10.22581/muet1982.1803.17. http://publications.muet.edu.pk/index.php/muetrj/article/view/511
6. Bibi, S., et al.: Requirement change management in global software environment using cloud computing. J. Softw. Eng. Appl. **7**(8), 694–699 (2014)
7. Capability Maturity Model Integration Product Team: CMMI for Development, Version 1.3. Technical report CMU/SEI-2010-TR-033, Software Engineering Institute, Carnegie Mellon University, Pittsburgh, PA (2010). http://resources.sei.cmu. edu/library/asset-view.cfm?AssetID=9661
8. Cocco, L., Mannaro, K., Concas, G.: A model for global software development with cloud platforms. In: 38th EUROMICRO Conference on Software Engineering and Advanced Applications (SEAA), Cesme, Izmir, Turkey, pp. 446–452, September 2012. https://doi.org/10.1109/SEAA.2012.67
9. Damian, D., Moitra, D.: Guest editors' introduction: global software development: how far have we come? IEEE Softw. **23**(5), 17–19 (2006). https://doi.org/10.1109/ MS.2006.126
10. Herbsleb, J., Moitra, D.: Global software development. IEEE Softw. **18**(2), 16–20 (2001). https://doi.org/10.1109/52.914732
11. Iliasov, A., et al.: Supporting reuse in event B development: modularisation approach. In: Frappier, M., Glässer, U., Khurshid, S., Laleau, R., Reeves, S. (eds.) ABZ 2010. LNCS, vol. 5977, pp. 174–188. Springer, Heidelberg (2010). https:// doi.org/10.1007/978-3-642-11811-1_14
12. Khan, A., Basri, S., Dominic, P.: A propose framework for requirement change management in global software development. In: 2012 International Conference on Computer Information Science (ICCIS), Kuala Lumpur, Malaysia, vol. 2, pp. 944–947, June 2012. https://doi.org/10.1109/ICCISci.2012.6297161
13. Kumar, S.A., Kumar, T.A.: Study the impact of requirements management characteristics in global software development projects: an ontology based approach. Int. J. Softw. Eng. Appl. **2**(4), 107 (2011)
14. Niazi, M., El-Attar, M., Usman, M., Ikram, N.: GlobReq: a framework for improving requirements engineering in global software development projects: preliminary results. In: 16th International Conference on Evaluation Assessment in Software Engineering (EASE 2012), pp. 166–170, May 2012. https://doi.org/10.1049/ic. 2012.0021

15. Object Management Group Inc.: Open Services for Lifecycle Collaboration (OSLC) (2019). http://open-services.net/

16. Pan, Y., Hu, N.: Research on dependability of cloud computing systems. In: 2014 International Conference on Reliability, Maintainability and Safety (ICRMS), Guangzhou, China, pp. 435–439, August 2014. https://doi.org/10.1109/ICRMS.2014.7107234

17. Project Management Institute: Adoption of the Project Management Institute (PMI) Standard: A Guide to the Project Management Body of Knowledge (PMBOK Guide)-2008 (4th edn.) IEEE P1490/D1, May 2011, pp. 1–505, June 2011. https://doi.org/10.1109/IEEESTD.2011.5937011

18. Ramasubbu, N., Balan, R.K.: Globally distributed software development project performance: an empirical analysis. In: Proceedings of the the 6th Joint Meeting of the European Software Engineering Conference and the ACM SIGSOFT Symposium on The Foundations of Software Engineering, ESEC-FSE 2007, pp. 125–134. ACM, New York (2007). https://doi.org/10.1145/1287624.1287643

Fault-Tolerant IoT
A Systematic Mapping Study

Mahyar Tourchi Moghaddam$^{(\boxtimes)}$ and Henry Muccini

University of L'Aquila, Via Vetoio 1, L'Aquila, Italy
{mahtou,henry.muccini}@univaq.it

Abstract. A failure may occur at all architectural levels of the Internet of Things (IoT) applications: sensor and actuator nodes can be missed, network links can be down, and processing and storage components can fail to perform properly. That is the reason for which fault-tolerance (FT) has become a crucial concern for IoT systems.

Our study aims at identifying and classifying the existing FT mechanisms that can tolerate the IoT systems failure. In line with a systematic mapping study selection procedure, we picked out 60 papers among over 2300 candidate studies. To this end, we applied a rigorous classification and extraction framework to select and analyze the most influential domain-related information. Our analysis revealed the following main findings: *(i)* whilst researchers tend to study fault-tolerant IoT (FT-IoT) in cloud level only, several studies extend the application to fog and edge computing; *(ii)* there is a growing scientific interest on using the microservices architecture to address FT in IoT systems; *(iii)* the IoT components distribution, collaboration and intelligent elements location impact the system resiliency. This study gives a foundation to classify the existing and future approaches for fault-tolerant IoT, by classifying a set of methods, techniques and architectures that are potentially capable to reduce IoT systems failure.

Keywords: Fault-tolerance · Internet of Things ·
Software architecture · Systematic mapping study

1 Introduction

IoT is the internal/external communication of intelligent elements via internet to provide smart services [1]. A dependable IoT system should provide reliable and fault-free services. A fault is a defect within the hardware or software systems that impacts the correct functionality. It is particularly difficult to establish a pattern for FT in IoT, since the IoT devices are heterogeneous, highly distributed, powered on battery, relied upon wireless communication and affected by scalability. The distribution of IoT devices cause the system to suffer from, e.g., server crash, server omission, incorrect response and arbitrary failure. The wireless and battery dependency makes the IoT devices barely recoverable. Furthermore, being exposed to new devices and services impacts the system performance.

© Springer Nature Switzerland AG 2019
R. Calinescu and F. Di Giandomenico (Eds.): SERENE 2019, LNCS 11732, pp. 67–84, 2019.
https://doi.org/10.1007/978-3-030-30856-8_5

Although the IoT has been introduced more than one decade ago, the research and industry communities are still trying to define its different aspects and Quality of Services (QoS) such as FT. Hence, the goal of this research is to identify and classify the domain state of the art and to highlight the methods, techniques and architectures that are potentially suitable to model a FT-IoT. In order to achieve this goal, a systematic mapping study has been performed. The primary studies have been chosen based on an accurate inclusion and exclusion criteria and a deep analysis. The main contributions of this study are: *(i)* addressing to an up to date state of the art class for Fault-tolerant IoT modeling, which can be used as a future research and implementation reference; *(ii)* investigating on an IoT reference architecture and assessing the impact of such a software design on FT; *(iii)* identifying current characteristics, challenges and publication trends with respect to FT-IoT approach.

The audience of this study are both research and industry communities interested to improve their knowledge and select suitable methods to design their IoT systems.

The paper is organized as follows. Section 2 reveals the design of this systematic study. Section 3 presents a reference IoT architecture and analyzes its associated FT aspects. Sections 4, 5, 6, 7 and 8 elaborate on the obtained results while Sect. 9 analyses threats to validity. Section 10 closes the paper and discusses future work.

2   Research Method

The goal of this research is formulated based on the Goal-Question-Metric perspectives [2,3] as follow:

> *Purpose*: to provide a deep understanding on Fault-tolerant IoT systems
> *Issue*: by identifying, classifying and analyzing different methods, techniques and architectures
> *Object*: based on existing IoT systems approaches
> *Viewpoint*: from both research and industry viewpoints.

2.1   Search Strategy

To achieve the aforementioned goal, we arranged for a set of questions:

- **RQ1:** *What IoT architectural styles and patterns are able to make the system prone to fault?*
- **RQ2:** *What traditional and novel techniques and methods can protect IoT systems against failure?*
- **RQ3:** *What are the quality attributes associated with Fault-tolerance in IoT systems?*
- **RQ4:** *What are the trends and evolution that can be deduced from the scientific publications on FT-IoT?*

Furthermore, a good search strategy should provide effective solutions to the following questions [4]:

Which approaches? The search strategy consists of two phases: *(i)* an automatic search on academic database; and *(ii)* a snowballing. The first step has been performed using the search string below. A selection criteria has been subsequently applied on the set of results. Then a snowballing procedure on the included results of the automatic search has been applied to structure the final set of primary studies.

(IoT OR "ternet of Things" OR "Internet-of-Things") AND ("Fault tolerant" OR "Fault-tolerant" OR "Fault tolerance" OR "Fault-tolerance")

Where to search? The electronic databases that we used for the automatic search (ACM, IEEE, Elsevier, Springer, ISI Web of Science, and Wiley Inter Science) are known as the main source of literature for potentially relevant studies on software engineering.

When and what time span to search? We did not consider publication year as a criterion for the search and selection steps. Thus, all studies coming from the selection steps, until May 2019, were included regardless of their publication time.

2.2 Selection Strategy

A multi-stage selection process (Fig. 1) has been designed to give a full control on the number and characteristics of the studies coming from different stages[1].

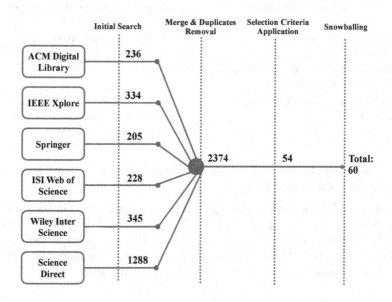

Fig. 1. Search and selection process.

---

[1] It is worth mentioning that we considered "Software Engineering" as the *Search Topic*, since the original search leaded to 193,000 results.

Afterwards, we considered all the selected studies, and filtered them according to a set of well-defined inclusion and exclusion criteria (Table 1). According to the standards, the definition of inclusion/ exclusion criteria has been guided by two main drivers: *(i)* keeping the focus of the selected papers on the scope of the study; and *(ii)* avoiding gray or not scientific works. Thus, Inclusion/exclusion criteria shall be aligned with the research questions. We included studies that satisfied all inclusion criteria, and discarded studies that met any exclusion criterion.

On the 2,374 potentially relevant papers, we performed a first manual step applying the selection criteria on title and abstract of the papers. Afterwards, a second manual step of reading the full text of firstly selected papers has been performed and followed by snowballing. The reasons for which we obtained only 60 primary studies over 2,374 potentially relevant papers are that: *(i)* our search string was quite inclusive (to avoid ignoring any potentially relevant paper); *(ii)* however, selection criteria application has been carefully performed in a way to avoid including the papers that fall out of the scope of the research. In order to minimize bias, the procedure has been performed by the first researcher and the results have been double-checked by the other researcher.

Table 1. Inclusion and exclusion criteria.

Inclusion criteria	Exclusion criteria
Studies that propose, leverage, or analyze software and hardware solutions, methods, techniques and architectures to design fault-tolerant IoT systems	Studies that, while focusing on IoT, do not focus on its fault-tolerance aspects (e.g., studies focusing only on technological aspects of IoT) or vice versa
Studies subject to peer review (e.g., journal papers, papers published as part of conference proceedings, workshop papers, and book chapters)	Secondary or tertiary studies (e.g., systematic literature reviews, surveys, etc.)
Studies written in English language and available in full-text	Studies in the form of tutorial papers, editorials, etc. because they do not provide enough information

After selection of a final set of primary studies, the data has been extracted to answer the research questions.

Study Replicability. A replication package is provided to tackle the page limits of a workshop paper: https://www.dropbox.com/s/ansb75ncdoqpc9f/DATA-SERENE-2019.xlsx?dl=0. The package is available as an excel file with different sheets that include all necessary information such as search results, primary studies distribution, data extraction and validity examination.

3   Background on IoT Architectures

In this section, we present a reference software architecture for the internet of things applications [5–7]. IoT applications typically consist of a set of software

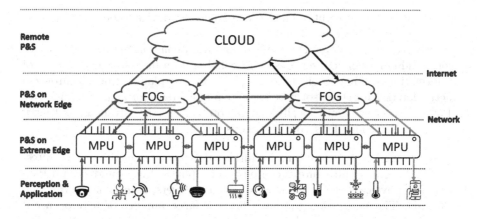

Fig. 2. IoT reference architecture (MPU refers to microprocessor unit).

components including perception, data processing and storage (P&S) and actuation, which are distributed across network(s). For the purposes of this paper that has its focus on fault-tolerant data transmission and analysis, we define our architecture based on the following P&S modeling characteristics:

- *Distribution*: this aspect specifies whether data analysis software ought to be deployed on a single node or on several nodes that are distributed across the IoT system. In other words, the distribution is referred to the deployment of the IoT P&S software to hardware. By using a distributed style, the latency will potentially be reduced due to data traffic and bandwidth consumption minimization. Such rapid response time facilitates real-time and fault-tolerant IoT applications. Furthermore, in distributed systems, a faulty P&S will still hold IoT system available since the faulty component can be replaced by another one.
- *Localization*: depending on data size and required analysis complexity, P&S can be executed locally or remotely. Here is the point in which centralized cloud and distributed edge and fog concepts become relevant. The advantage of using a central cloud is that, processing on a cloud component facilitates long-term data analysis for systems that have no constraints on response time. For applications with massive P&S requirement, executing the task on the powerful cloud is the only solution.

  Fog nodes are the intermediate P&S, which bring a degree of cloud functionality to the network edge. Fog is not limited to perform on a particular device, so that it can freely be located between device edge and cloud. The analysis capacity of fog is lower than cloud, but it reduces a significant point of failure by shifting towards more than one computational component. However, fog only performs locally so that it does not have a global coverage over a major IoT system. It is worth mentioning that, some IoT devices are able to perform simple P&S by themselves. Performing P&S on IoT device edge, refers to computation capabilities embedded on a smart device to be able to gather and analyze environmental data.

- *Collaboration*: the aforementioned computation components may interact to form and empower IoT services. This collaboration may appear as a level of information sharing, coordinated analysis and/or planning or synchronized actuation. Each IoT sensor network may provide data for many collaborative P&S components, both locally and remotely. Here the advantage is that if the local P&S node fails, local service is still in access.

Considering above definitions, we further design our reference IoT architecture (Fig. 2). The architecture is composed of a physical layer and several P&S layers. The physical layer is made up of two sub-layers, namely *perception* and *application*. The perception sub-layer hosts a large number of heterogeneous sensors and the application sub-layer consists of various types of actuators. The P&S layers store and analyze data gathered by the perception components to provide the required IoT service.

Looking through primary studies, each of them address the FT for specific layer(s) of the IoT architecture. As shown in Fig. 3, whilst the faults usually occur in sense (26/60) and actuation (12/60) sub-layers, the primary studies realized the importance of network (38/60) and P&S (33/60) layers for FT-IoT systems. The reason is that, handling FT is under the responsibility of P&S nodes and is based on the transmitted data coming from the physical layer. In Sect. 5, we discuss various FT strategies and techniques for IoT systems.

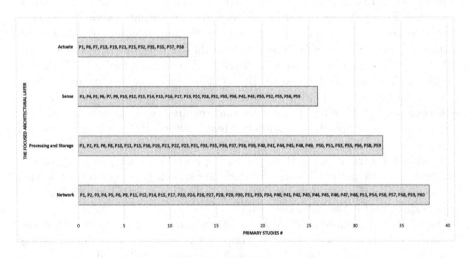

Fig. 3. The primary studies focus on each architectural layer.

4   Fault-Tolerant IoT Architectural Patterns and Styles (RQ1)

This section discusses the specific characteristics of primary studies related to FT-IoT architectural design. The primary studies used one or more overlaid style(s) to design their software system. However, among the various IoT architectural styles, layered architecture (32/60) was the clear winner as reported in Fig. 4. In the layered view the system is viewed as a complex heterogeneous entity that can be decomposed into interacting parts. The primary studies designed their layered architecture in different ways, ranged from 3 (with a central P&S component only) to 5 (including edge and fog) layers (see Fig. 2).

Cloud-based architecture (28/60) won the second position. Fog that is a significant extension to cloud environment is addressed in 15 studies as well. Few studies (4/60) used the device edge concept to design their FT-IoT architecture. Minimizing the impact of a failed component within an integrated fog-cloud platform needs a common agreement protocol that is able to uniform the system with the minimum rounds of message exchange.

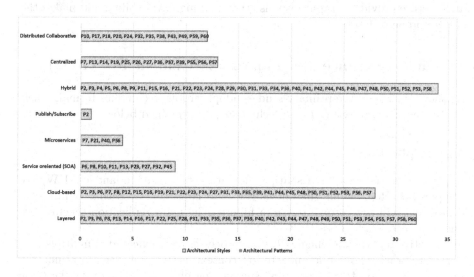

Fig. 4. FT-IoT architectural styles and patterns.

Service oriented architectures (SOA) (9/60) put the service at the centre of their IoT application design. In fact, the core application component makes the service available for other IoT components over a network. Microservices (4/60) and SOA have the same goal in IoT sytems, that is building one or multiple applications from a set of different services. A microservice is a small application with single responsibility, which can be deployed, scaled and tested independently.

P21 proposes a pluggable framework based on a microservices architecture that implements FT support as two complementary microservices: one that uses complex event processing for real-time FT detection, and another that uses online machine learning to detect fault patterns and preemptively mitigate faults before they are activated. P7 propose a system based on container virtualisation that allows IoT clouds to carry out fault-tolerance when a microservice running on an IoT device fails. A reactive microservices architecture and its application in a fog computing case study to investigate FT challenges at the edge of the network is presented in P40. P56 present a microservices-based mobile cloud platform by exploiting containerization which replaces heavyweight virtual machines to guarantee run-time FT.

On the other hand, as explained in Sect. 3, IoT distribution patterns classify the architectures according to edge intelligence and elements collaboration. Figure 4 shows the distribution patterns that are used by the primary studies. Most of studies used a Hybrid pattern (34/60) followed by the Centralized (13/60) and the Distributed Collaborative (12/60) patterns.

In this section we showed that edge/cloud-based distributed architectures are extensively used by primary studies. The results confirm that: a distributed architecture provides a rapid response time and high availability, and makes the system prone to fault.

5   Fault-Tolerance Techniques for Resilient IoT (RQ2)

As shown in Fig. 5, the primary studies adopt various techniques to make their IoT system fault-tolerant. These techniques are explained below.

5.1   Replication

Replication is the process of sharing the data between redundant IoT HW/SW components. Replication guarantees the data consistency, so that failure of a component will not result in system failure. The main replication schemes are known as *active and passive* [8].

In active replication scheme (22/60), processes are replicated in multiple processors to provide fault-tolerance. In IoT context, active replication continuously pushes the group of IoT resources (such as fog or cloud) to execute the same process concurrently. In case of fault, failover can have in very short period to other active resources [P33]. In this way, an extra processing is occurred and redundant and duplicated dataset it sent to endpoint. Despite that active replication takes a lot of processing resources, it is failure transparent and its failure discovery time is deterministic.

In passive replication (24/60), the primary processor performs and the extra IoT components remain idle until a failure occurs. The idle components, however, contact the primary processor in order to be updated and keep consistency. The passive replication scheme imposes additional cost of resources and suffers from slow response to failure.

5.2   Network Control

In network control scheme (19/60), the IoT network is generally divided into various clusters. A chosen cluster head (CH) periodically makes roll call requests to the other nodes and if it does not receive a reply message, the failure will be confirmed. However, the CH itself makes a single point of failure. Several cluster-based routing protocols have been proposed by the primary studies. Some primary studies took advantage of bio-inspired particle multi-swarm optimization routing algorithm to construct, recover, and select disjoint paths that tolerate the failure while satisfying the quality of service parameters. Some other studies used the virtual CH formation and flow graph modeling to efficiently tolerate the failures of CHs. Multiple traveling salesman is also among the routing algorithms that are addressed by the primary studies.

5.3   Distributed Recovery Block

In this method (8/60), a single program is concurrently executed on a node pair, from which one is active and the other is inactive. In no-fault situation, the main (active) node performs the task and the other node performs the same task in shadow. Afterwards, both results will be tested and if the test is properly passed, the results associated with the main node will be delivered as the output. If the primary node test fails, the shadow node becomes active and produces the outputs. This method can protect the system only against a single point of failure.

5.4   Time Redundancy

Time redundancy (1/60) can be performed at both instruction and task levels. At instruction level, the program is duplicated and subsequently the results are compared to discover a potential error. In task level, a software is run twice (or more) to mitigate dynamic faults. Despite that this method does not impose the cost of additional hardware, it increases the time needed to assure redundancy. The method reduces the computing performance and consumes more energy as well.

It is worth mentioning that, the whole IoT system can follow a *Reactive* or *Proactive* strategy. Reactive FT starts to recover the system after the detection of an error (using event processing methods). In proactive FT, the recovery strategy is started even before the detection of an error (using machine learning methods).

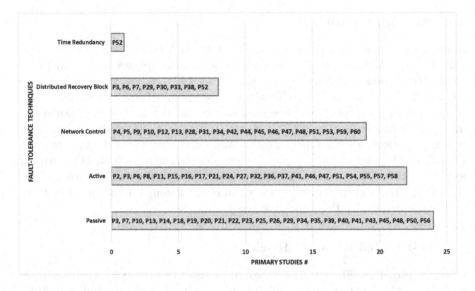

Fig. 5. Fault-tolerance techniques.

6   Quality of IoT Service Associated with Fault-Tolerance (RQ3)

The standard used to categorize quality attributes comes from ISO 25010 and some specific IoT attributes derived from the primary studies keywording.

An IoT system brings many challenges from QoS perspective when takes into account FT. As shown in Fig. 6, the most recognized quality challenges

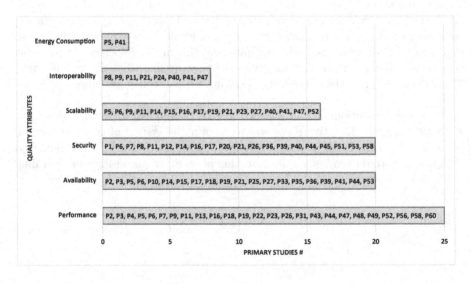

Fig. 6. QoS associated with FT-IoT.

are related to performance (25/60), availability (20/60), security (20/60) and scalability (16/60), whilst interoperability (8/60) and energy efficiency (2/60) are positioned in a lower degree of concern.

The level of performance depends on how much the processing and storage components are pushed to the edge in a decentralized way. Availability is the ability of a system to be fully or partly operational as and when required. Clearly, FT and availability are not identical since a fault-tolerant system is supposed to maintain the system operational without interruption, but a highly available system may have service interruption. However, A fault-tolerant system should maintain a high level of system availability and performance as well.

In IoT systems that different components and entities are connected to each other through a network, security gains a high concern. Scalability is also an essential attribute as IoT systems should be capable to perform properly considering a huge number of heterogeneous devices. Commenting on scalability of IoT as a whole system is difficult, however, it depends on how new resources can be added on demand. A fault-tolerant system also requires enormous computational efforts to be run in distributed P&S components. Device heterogeneity and P&S elements distribution make the system resistive to scalability.

Interoperability helps IoT heterogeneous components to work together efficiently. It actually depends on how much IoT large-scale heterogeneous devices can communicate directly among each other to gather the required data without having to go through the central/remote components. Since most of IoT devices are battery powered, energy efficiency that is tied to many other quality attributes (such as performance) becomes essential. However, wireless and battery dependency make the IoT devices barely recoverable, flexible to scalability and performant.

7   Horizontal Analysis

This section reports the results orthogonal to the vertical analysis presented in the previous sections. For the purpose of this section, we cross-tabulated and grouped the data, we made comparisons between pairs of concepts of our classification framework and identified perspectives of interest.

7.1   FT Techniques vs Architectural Patterns

Here the question is, *which architectural pattern is more often used for each FT technique?* As shown in Fig. 7, (11/60) studies used hybrid pattern to facilitate their passive FT techniques, whilst (15/60) used hybrid for active FT. In contrary, centralized and collaborative architectural patterns are more suitable to address passive FT. Obviously, network control FT technique is better to be addressed by a hybrid architectural pattern. In general, a hybrid architecture guarantees FT-IoT, since if one fog node fails, the IoT system can shift the computation to another fog to avoid the single point of failure.

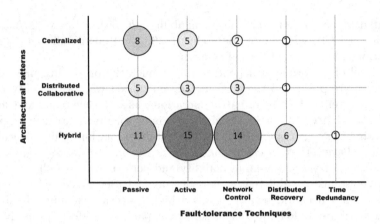

Fig. 7. FT techniques vs patterns.

7.2   FT Techniques vs Quality Attributes

What quality attributes are satisfied when a specific FT technique is adopted?
As shown in Fig. 8, passive technique mostly takes into account performance
and availability, whilst the active technique gives more weight to security and

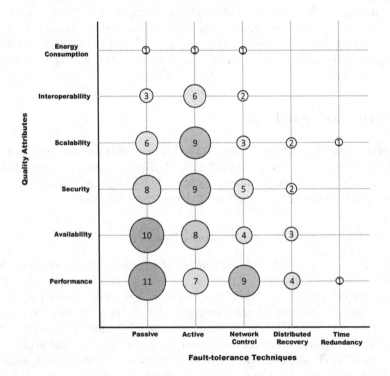

Fig. 8. Techniques vs quality attributes.

scalability. Furthermore, network control enhances the performance beside the fault-tolerance. Regarding the rapid development and extension of devices in the edge of the network, performance of IoT should be maintained in an appropriate level. Performance highly depends on the data storage and application logic distribution among edge and central servers. As mentioned before, fog computing can pave the way to improve IoT systems performance level.

8   Challenges and Emerging Trends (RQ4)

In this section the emerging trends in resilience for FT-IoT are presented. To this end, publication year, type and venue are firstly extracted and an overall discussion is subsequently provided.

8.1   Publication Year

Figure 9 shows the distribution of FT-IoT literature. It noticeably indicates that the number of papers grows by time and there is just one related paper published before 2014. This result confirms the scientific interest and research necessity on FT-IoT issues in the last few years.

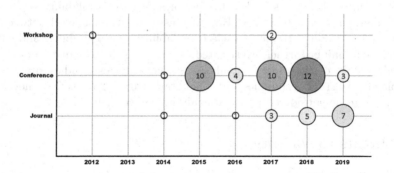

Fig. 9. Primary studies distribution by publication type.

8.2   Publication Type

The most common publication type is conference paper (40/60), followed by journal (17/60), and workshop paper (3/60). Such a high number of journal and conference papers may point out that FT-IoT is maturing as a research topic despite that it is still relatively young.

8.3   Publication Venues

From the extracted data we can notice that research on FT-IoT is spread across many venues mostly in the span of IoT (e.g. WF-IoT), computing (e.g. ICAC) and networking (e.g. ICOIN) communities. The complete list of venues can be found in the data extraction file. However, the focus on the aforementioned aspects can prove the significance of distributed computing and networking for FT-IoT systems.

8.4   Emerging Trends in Resilience for FT-IoT

Our study reveals that some of the different Ft-IoT techniques are more rarely covered with respect to others, specifically, distributed recovery block and time redundancy. We clarify that this result by no means implies that there is limited literature or support on such FT techniques, but they appear to have a more limited application on IoT. In architectural level, we observed a significant move toward adopting hybrid architectures, which make the IoT system prone to fault. Furthermore, whilst a growth on using service-oriented and microservices architectures is perceived, their various aspects need to be better investigated regarding FT. The study showed that for FT-IoT architectural layers, the attention especially goes to network and processing and storage components.

What our study reveals is also that performance and availability are tied up with IoT systems fault-tolerance. However, assessing the trade-off between FT and other IoT quality attributes such as scalability, interoperability and energy consumption shall be further investigated. Another result to be further evaluated through a state of the practice analysis, is that only few studies support the interplay between FT techniques and collaborative architectures. The mentioned aspects are to be considered by the domain future work.

9   Threats to Validity

According to Peterson et al. [9], the quality rating for this systematic mapping study assessed and scored as 73%. This value is the ratio of the number of actions taken in comparison to the total number of actions reported in the quality checklist. The quality score of our study is far beyond the scores obtained by existing systematic mapping studies in the literature, which have a distribution with a median of 33% and 48% as absolute maximum value. However, the threats to validity are unavoidable. Below we shortly define the main threats to validity of our study and the way we mitigated them.

External validity: in our study, the most severe threat related to external validity may consist of having a set of primary studies that is not representative of the whole research on FT-IoT. We mitigated this potential threat by *(i)* following a search strategy including both automatic search and backward-forward snowballing of selected studies; and *(ii)* defining a set of inclusion and exclusion criteria. Along the same lines, gray and non-English literature are not included in our research as we want to focus exclusively on the state of the art presented in high-quality scientific studies in English.

Internal validity: it refers to the level of influence that extraneous variables may have on the design of the study. We mitigated this potential threat to validity by *(i)* rigorously defining and validating the structure of our study, *(ii)* defining our classification framework by carefully following the keywording process, and *(iii)* conducting a well-structured vertical analysis. Construct validity: It concerns the validity of extracted data with respect to the research questions. We mitigated this potential source of threats in different ways. *(i)* performing automatic search on a couple of databases to avoid potential biases; *(ii)* having a strong and tested search string; *(iii)* complementing the automatic by the snowballing activity; and *(iv)* rigorously screen the studies according to inclusion and exclusion criteria.

Conclusion validity: it concerns the relationship between the extracted data and the obtained results. We mitigated potential threats to conclusion validity by applying well accepted systematic methods and processes throughout our study and documenting all of them in the excel package.

10   Conclusion

In this paper we present a systematic mapping study with the goal of classifying and identifying the domain state-of-the-art and extract a set of FT-IoT methods and techniques. Starting from over 2300 potentially relevant studies, we applied a rigorous selection procedure resulting in 60 primary studies. The results of this study are both research and industry oriented and are intended to make a framework for future research in FT-IoT related fields. As a future work, we will assess the potential integration of existing research to an industrial level of IoT.

Primary Studies

- **P1:** Toward a New Approach to IoT Fault Tolerance, https://doi.org/10.1109/MC.2016.238
- **P2:** CEFIoT: A fault-tolerant IoT architecture for edge and cloud, https://doi.org/10.1109/WF-IoT.2018.8355149
- **P3:** Reliable and Fault-Tolerant IoT-Edge Architecture, https://doi.org/10.1109/ICSENS.2018.8589624
- **P4:** Efficient Fault-Tolerant Routing in IoT Wireless Sensor Networks Based on Bipartite-Flow Graph Modeling, https://doi.org/10.1109/ACCESS.2019.2894002
- **P5:** Optimizing Multipath Routing With Guaranteed Fault Tolerance in Internet of Things, https://doi.org/10.1109/JSEN.2017.2739188
- **P6:** Brume - A Horizontally Scalable and Fault Tolerant Building Operating System, https://doi.org/10.1109/IoTDI.2018.00018
- **P7:** A Watchdog Service Making Container-Based Micro-services Reliable in IoT Clouds, https://doi.org/10.1109/FiCloud.2017.57

- **P8:** Towards Fault Tolerant Fog Computing for IoT-Based Smart City Applications, https://doi.org/10.1109/CCWC.2019.8666447
- **P9:** Device clustering for fault monitoring in Internet of Things systems, https://doi.org/10.1109/WF-IoT.2015.7389057
- **P10:** Decentralized fault tolerance mechanism for intelligent IoT/M2M middleware, https://doi.org/10.1109/WF-IoT.2014.6803115
- **P11:** Application of Blockchain in Collaborative Internet-of-Things Services, https://doi.org/10.1109/TCSS.2019.2913165
- **P12:** A Review of Aggregation Algorithms for the Internet of Things, https://doi.org/10.1109/ICSEng.2017.43
- **P13:** Supporting Service Adaptation in Fault Tolerant Internet of Things, https://doi.org/10.1109/SOCA.2015.38
- **P14:** Fault tolerant and scalable IoT-based architecture for health monitoring, https://doi.org/10.1109/SAS.2015.7133626
- **P15:** Fault tolerance capability of cloud data center, https://doi.org/10.1109/ICCP.2017.8117053
- **P16:** Reaching Agreement in an Integrated Fog Cloud IoT, https://doi.org/10.1109/ACCESS.2018.2877609
- **P17:** Byzantine Resilient Protocol for the IoT, https://doi.org/10.1109/JIOT.2018.2871157
- **P18:** DRAW: Data Replication for Enhanced Data Availability in IoT-based Sensor Systems, https://doi.org/10.1109/DASC/PiCom/DataCom
- **P19:** Power efficient, bandwidth optimized and fault tolerant sensor management for IOT in Smart Home, https://doi.org/10.1109/IADCC.2015.7154732
- **P20:** Energy efficiency and robustness for IoT: Building a smart home security system, https://doi.org/10.1109/ICCP.2016.7737120
- **P21:** A Microservices Architecture for Reactive and Proactive Fault Tolerance in IoT Systems, https://doi.org/10.1109/WoWMoM.2018.8449789
- **P22:** Management of solar energy in microgrids using IoT-based dependable control, https://doi.org/10.1109/ICEMS.2017.8056441
- **P23:** A hierarchical cloud architecture for integrated mobility, service, and trust management of service-oriented IoT systems, https://doi.org/10.1109/INTECH.2016.7845021
- **P24:** Fault-Tolerant Real-Time Collaborative Network Edge Analytics for Industrial IoT and Cyber Physical Systems with Communication Network Diversity, https://doi.org/10.1109/CIC.2018.00052
- **P25:** Fault-Tolerant mHealth Framework in the Context of IoT-Based Real-Time Wearable Health Data Sensors, https://doi.org/10.1109/ACCESS.2019.2910411
- **P26:** SCONN: Design and Implement Dual-Band Wireless Networking Assisted Fault Tolerant Data Transmission in Intelligent Buildings, https://doi.org/10.1109/VTCFall.2018.8690787
- **P27:** Fault-tolerant application placement in heterogeneous cloud environments, https://doi.org/10.1109/CNSM.2015.7367359
- **P28:** A reliable and energy efficient IoT data transmission scheme for smart cities based on redundant residue based error correction coding, https://doi.org/10.1109/SECONW.2015.7328141
- **P29:** Distributed Continuous-Time Fault Estimation Control for Multiple Devices in IoT Networks, https://doi.org/10.1109/ACCESS.2019.2892905
- **P30:** Trend-adaptive multi-scale PCA for data fault detection in IoT networks, https://doi.org/10.1109/ICOIN.2018.8343217

- **P31:** Adaptive and Fault-tolerant Data Processing in Healthcare IoT Based on Fog Computing, https://doi.org/10.1109/TNSE.2018.2859307
- **P32:** Fault-Recovery and Coherence in Internet of Things Choreographies, https://doi.org/10.1109/WF-IoT.2014.6803224
- **P33:** A Novel Data Reduction Technique with Fault-tolerance for Internet-of-things, https://doi.org/10.1145/3018896.3018971
- **P34:** Performance Comparisons of Fault-Tolerant Rouging Approaches for IoT Wireless Sensor Networks, https://doi.org/10.1145/3195106.3195168
- **P35:** Rivulet: A Fault-tolerant Platform for Smart-home Applications, https://doi.org/10.1145/3135974.3135988
- **P36:** Censorship Resistant Decentralized IoT Management Systems, https://doi.org/10.1145/3286978.3286979
- **P37:** Towards a Foundation for a Collaborative Replicable Smart Cities IoT Architecture, https://doi.org/10.1145/3063386.3063763
- **P38:** Responsible Objects: Towards Self-Healing Internet of Things Applications, https://doi.org/10.1109/ICAC.2015.60
- **P39:** A Multi-agent System Architecture for Self-Healing Cloud Infrastructure, https://doi.org/10.1145/2896387.2896392
- **P40:** Reactive Microservices for the Internet of Things: A Case Study in Fog Computing, https://doi.org/10.1145/3297280.3297402
- **P41:** Fault Tolerance Techniques and Architectures in Cloud Computing - a Comparative Analysis, https://doi.org/10.1109/ICGCIoT.2015.7380625
- **P42:** Energy Efficient Fault-tolerant Clustering Algorithm for Wireless Sensor Networks, https://doi.org/10.1109/ICGCIoT.2015.7380464
- **P43:** Layered Fault Management Scheme for End-to-end Transmission in Internet of Things, https://doi.org/10.1007/s11036-012-0355-5
- **P44:** An Architectural Mechanism for Resilient IoT Services, https://doi.org/10.1145/3137003.3137010
- **P45:** Resilience of Stateful IoT Applications in a Dynamic Fog Environment, https://doi.org/10.1145/3286978.3287007
- **P46:** The Optimal Generalized Byzantine Agreement in Cluster-based Wireless Sensor Networks, https://doi.org/10.1016/j.csi.2014.01.005
- **P47:** A Reliable IoT System for Personal Healthcare Devices, https://doi.org/10.1016/j.future.2017.04.004
- **P48:** Reliable Industrial IoT-based Distributed Automation, https://doi.org/10.1145/3302505.3310072
- **P49:** Low-Cost Memory Fault Tolerance for IoT Devices, https://doi.org/10.1145/3126534
- **P50:** Idea: A System for Efficient Failure Management in Smart IoT Environments, https://doi.org/10.1145/2906388.2906406
- **P51:** Patterns for Things That Fail, https://www.hillside.net/plop/2017/papers/proceedings/papers/07-ramadas.pdf
- **P52:** Fall-curve: A Novel Primitive for IoT Fault Detection and Isolation, https://doi.org/10.1145/3274783.3274853
- **P53:** Multilevel IoT Model for Smart Cities Resilience, https://doi.org/10.1145/3095786.3095793
- **P54:** Energy Efficient Device Discovery for Reliable Communication in 5G-based IoT and BSNs Using Unmanned Aerial Vehicles, https://doi.org/10.1016/j.jnca.2017.08.013
- **P55:** A Programming Framework for Implementing Fault-Tolerant Mechanism in IoT Applications, https://doi.org/10.1007/978-3-319-27137-8_56

- **P56:** Transient fault aware application partitioning computational offloading algorithm in microservices based mobile cloudlet networks, https://doi.org/10.1007/s00607-019-00733-4
- **P57:** Channel Dependability of the ATM Communication Network Based on the Multilevel Distributed Cloud Technology, https://doi.org/10.1007/978-3-319-67642-5_49
- **P58:** Design of compressed sensing fault-tolerant encryption scheme for key sharing in IoT Multi-cloudy environment(s), https://doi.org/10.1016/j.jisa.2019.04.004
- **P59:** Fault-Tolerant Temperature Control Algorithm for IoT Networks in Smart Buildings, https://doi.org/10.3390/en11123430
- **P60:** Virtualization in Wireless Sensor Networks: Fault Tolerant Embedding for Internet of Things, https://doi.org/10.1109/JIOT.2017.2717704

References

1. Muccini, H., Moghaddam, M.T.: IoT architectural styles. In: Cuesta, C.E., Garlan, D., Pérez, J. (eds.) ECSA 2018. LNCS, vol. 11048, pp. 68–85. Springer, Cham (2018). https://doi.org/10.1007/978-3-030-00761-4_5
2. Kitchenham, B., Brereton, P.: A systematic review of systematic review process research in software engineering. Inf. Softw. Technol. **55**(12), 2049–2075 (2013)
3. Kitchenham, B.A., Charters, S.: Guidelines for performing systematic literature reviews in software engineering. Technical report, EBSE-2007-01 (2007)
4. Zhang, H., Babar, M.A., Tell, P.: Identifying relevant studies in software engineering. Inf. Softw. Technol. **53**(6), 625–637 (2011). https://doi.org/10.1016/j.infsof.2010.12.010
5. Muccini, H., Spalazzese, R., Moghaddam, M.T., Sharaf, M.: Self-adaptive IoT architectures: an emergency handling case study. In: Proceedings of the 12th European Conference on Software Architecture: Companion Proceedings, p. 19. ACM (2018)
6. Muccini, H., Arbib, C., Davidsson, P., Tourchi Moghaddam, M.: An IoT software architecture for an evacuable building architecture. In: Proceedings of the 52nd Hawaii International Conference on System Sciences (2019)
7. Arbib, C., Arcelli, D., Dugdale, J., Moghaddam, M., Muccini, H.: Real-time emergency response through performant IoT architectures. In: International Conference on Information Systems for Crisis Response and Management (ISCRAM) (2019)
8. Fayyaz, M., Vladimirova, T.: Survey and future directions of fault-tolerant distributed computing on board spacecraft. Adv. Space Res. **58**(11), 2352–2375 (2016)
9. Petersen, K., Vakkalanka, S., Kuzniarz, L.: Guidelines for conducting systematic mapping studies in software engineering: an update. Inf. Softw. Technol. **64**, 1–18 (2015)

JARVIS, A Hardware/Software Framework for Resilient Industry 4.0 Systems

Jacopo Parri⬥, Fulvio Patara⬥, Samuele Sampietro⬥,
and Enrico Vicario(✉)⬥

Department of Information Engineering, University of Florence, Florence, Italy
{jacopo.parri,fulvio.patara,samuele.sampietro,enrico.vicario}@unifi.it

Abstract. JARVIS is a Research & Development project, jointly developed by industrial SME partners and by the University of Florence, aimed at development of a hardware/software framework supporting integration among physical IoT devices, data analytic software agents, and human operators involved in operation and maintenance of resilient Industry 4.0 systems. At the heart of the JARVIS architecture, a suite of software digital twins deployed in a Java EE environment supports runtime monitoring and control of the hierarchy of hardware configuration items of the system, capturing their composition and representing their failure modes through a reflection architectural pattern enabling agile adaptation to the evolution of configurations. Besides, analytic modules can be deployed as micro-services leveraging both the knowledge base provided by digital twins and the data flowing from the ingestion layer. This enables agile development of advanced monitoring and control services supporting maintainability and resilience. We describe the JARVIS architecture, outlining responsibilities and collaborations among its modules, and we provide details on the structure of representation of digital twins, showing how this is exploited in a data analytic agent providing an executable representation of fault trees associated with failure modes of configuration items.

Keywords: I4.0 System of Systems · Digital twins · Fault tree

1 Introduction

In the agenda of Industry 4.0 (I4.0), Information Technology and Operational Technology are expected to provide facilities for conduction and maintenance of cyber-physical systems, developing on various pillars, including industrial IoT, big data and analytics, horizontal and vertical integration, cloud computing [23]. This gives rise to a class of software controlled distributed systems, for which resilience comprises a core requirement [1,19,24] shaping software engineering processes and architectural solutions.

R. Calinescu and F. Di Giandomenico (Eds.): SERENE 2019, LNCS 11732, pp. 85–93, 2019.
https://doi.org/10.1007/978-3-030-30856-8_6

JARVIS (Just-in-time ARtificial intelligence for the eValuation of Industrial Signals) is a project co-funded by the Tuscany regional government (Italy) in the POR FESR 2014–2020 program, developed by the industrial SME partners LASCAUX, SISMIC SISTEMI, JAEWA, and BEENOMIO, with the scientific support of the labs of Software Technologies, Artificial Intelligence, and Global Optimization of the University of Florence.

JARVIS aims at developing a hardware/software framework for integration, operation, and maintenance of Industry 4.0 systems, leveraging a software architecture that facilitates interaction among physical IoT devices, enterprise scale software agents, data analytics, and human operators, so as to support planning and scheduling of predictive maintenance and assets analysis, both offline and at runtime. On the one hand, a suite of software digital twins [25] deployed in the domain logic of a Java EE environment mirrors the hierarchical structure of physical devices in an IoT layer, enabling runtime monitoring and control of system hardware configuration items. On the other hand, a variety of data analytics and software agents drives agile development of advanced monitoring and control services for maintainability and resilience.

The project develops a framework open to reuse in the general context of Industry 4.0 systems, and validates its applicability through a concrete instance in a real operative scenario, addressing the case of a gate system for speed control and access regulation to limited traffic zones (ZTL), produced and manufactured by SISMIC SISTEMI, and installed in several Italian municipalities.

In this paper, we report a general description of the JARVIS project, outlining its major requirements (Sect. 2) and describing the architecture as a System of Systems (Sect. 3), and we then provide details, focusing on the structure of representation of digital twins and showing how this is exploited in a microservice providing an executable representation of fault trees associated with failure modes of configuration items (Sect. 4). Conclusions are drawn in Sect. 5.

2 System Requirements Specification

JARVIS is an architecture-driven project, developed along a V-model process [9], documented according to the MIL-STD-498 [20].

Main system requirements and their consequent structural choices include: *(i)* the system must be able to ingest Big Data from a plethora of IoT devices, which led to the adoption of an IoT broker; *(ii)* the system must manage the persistence of raw and semi-structured data into a high capacity data-store, which led to the adoption of a schema-less NoSQL column-oriented DBMS [12]; *(iii)* the system must promote inversion of responsibility, by allowing actions and end-users notifications be triggered by edge and unmanned components on occurrence of faulty conditions; *(iv)* the system must provide an executable software representation of physical field devices with monitoring capabilities, which led to the design of a digital twins domain logic; *(v)* the system must exhibit elasticity in scaling up/down the computational power of single modules, which led to a micro-service oriented architecture [6]; *(vi)* the system must

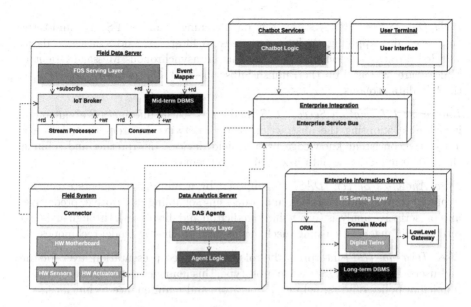

Fig. 1. UML deployment diagram of JARVIS architecture as a System of Systems.

be able to integrate applications, horizontally and vertically, along the production chain and among domains of authority, clients, customers, and tertiary manufacturers, which led to the adoption of Enterprise Application Integration (EAI) principles [15]; *(vii)* the system must integrate a swarm of data analytics and agents, supporting operations management and just-in-time maintenance processes, developed independently by different parties through paradigms of polyglot programming and polyglot persistence; *(viii)* the system must support push communications, providing an alternative multi-platform user interface, which led to the adoption of an ecosystem of chatbots [5].

In the specific focus of this paper, requirements *(iv)* and *(vii)* play a major role in the discussion.

3   System/Subsystem Design Description

JARVIS is developed around a System of Systems architecture (see Fig. 1), designed so as to promote high-levels of data ingestion, fault-tolerance, portability, and adaptability. Roles and responsibilities of subsystems are here explained in the general perspective of the project.

Field System (FS) acquires and generates IoT data flows, playing the role of perception layer [14] of an IoT architectural stack. An FS instance is a physical device composed of hardware components (e.g. motherboard, sensors and actuators) and software controllers (e.g. embedded firmware). In the JARVIS specific prototype, each FS represents a ZTL gate.

Field Data Server (FDS) stores raw data coming from the FS in a mid-term database, also applying analytic processes to filter, fix, and synthesise data. The IoT broker component, which acts as an asynchronous Message Oriented Middleware [3] based on the Publish-Subscribe EIP [13], performs ingestion of the IoT data streams.

Enterprise Information Server (EIS) maintains status information about monitored FSs, adopting the abstraction of digital twins, in order to maintain a long-term consistent knowledge base of field devices, interpreting and refining the mid-term FDS raw-data into a high level semantics.

Data Analytics Server (DAS) is composed by a plurality of agents executing dynamic context interpretation and processing, enabling descriptive, predictive, and prescriptive analysis (e.g. failure prediction and diagnoses), through artificial intelligence, machine learning mechanisms, and stochastic model techniques.

User Terminal (UT) interprets the role of decoupled presentation layer for the end-users. In the JARVIS specific prototype, this manages municipal authorities, municipal police officers, help desk operators and maintenance technicians.

Chatbot Services (CS) implements the internal logic of real-time messaging assistants, so as to expose an alternative UI which allows both push and pull duplex communications among human operators and physical devices, enabling inversion of responsibility mechanisms (i.e. machine-to-human and machine-to-machine interactions).

Enterprise Integration (EI) is responsible of subsystems interoperability, orchestrates services, and handles dynamic dependencies, authorizing and securing accesses to field devices. The core component is represented by the Enterprise Service Bus (ESB) [2], which guarantees high decoupling and push communications, also implementing some major micro-services patterns [16] to enhance availability and reliability, notably including: Circuit Breakers to limit fault propagations, Service Discovery and Gateways to route messages.

Overall, all these subsystems give rise to a so-called Lambda architecture [18], where the EIS implements the *batch layer*, the FDS serves as the *speed layer*, and the FDS, EIS and DAS jointly represent the *serving layer*. In the specific focus of this paper, EIS and DAS are the subsystems which cover the requirements *(iv)* and *(vii)*, respectively.

4   Digital Twins as Knowledge Base

The combination of EIS and DAS comprises a Knowledge Base supporting monitoring and control of resilience: the EIS provides a digital representation of structure and components of managed physical devices; besides the DAS hosts a variety of micro-services supporting operation and maintenance processes.

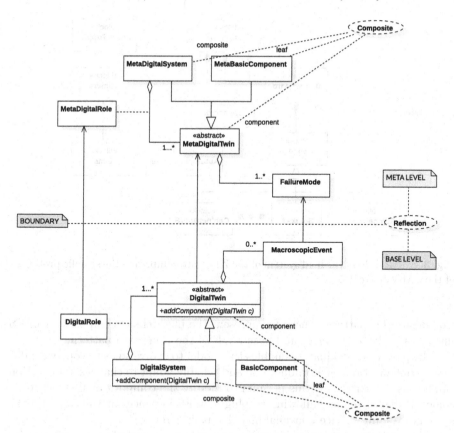

Fig. 2. UML class diagram of the domain model of EIS, showing the reflective and composite structure of digital twins. The association class *DigitalRole* (and its counterpart in the meta level) has been introduced to support same-typed and reusable components among different instances of *DigitalSystem* (and *MetaDigitalSystem*).

4.1 EIS Subsystem

The EIS subsystem is based on a domain logic, explicitly oriented toward reliability requirement, and populated by digital twins instances, whose focus is on capturing significant macroscopic events and failure modes, exhibited by whole physical systems or devices. Digital twin abstraction enables a two-way interaction on physical counterparts providing an interface to collect and query telemetries as well as to control remote actuators (e.g. reset command).

The domain model, depicted in Fig. 2, combines two software design patterns. The Reflection [22] pattern provides a mechanism to modify dynamically, at runtime, the structure and behaviour of modeled digital twins, by splitting the domain logic in two parts: the meta level captures the types of devices and their interconnections; the base level identifies concrete instances of physical components and their interfaces in the actual configuration of the system. Besides, the

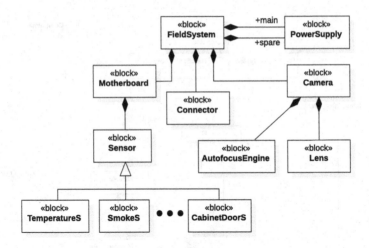

Fig. 3. SysML bdd of the field system of the ZTL gate comprising the specific prototype of the JARVIS project.

Composite [11] pattern is used to represent the hierarchical compositions of FS instances, in both the meta and base levels of the Reflection pattern.

The patterns combination enables the model to evolve so as to cope with different configurations of a product line and reliably adapt to changes in operation conditions. In particular, this permits to modify the compositional structure of some FS digital replica, allowing to plug new FS instances at runtime into the system, avoiding service unavailability due to EIS reboot.

The resulting software architecture promotes an engineering process where a specification of the structure of the system can be translated into an executable representation made of software digital twins.

Figure 3 illustrates the concept with reference to the configuration of the FS of a ZTL gate, here modeled as a SysML [10] Block Definition Diagram (bdd). Each block element of the bdd results into a *DigitalTwin* instance at runtime: basic and composed blocks are implemented as objects of type *BasicComponent* and *DigitalSystem*, respectively; *DigitalTwin* components of a *DigitalSystem* and their *DigitalRoles* can be derived from compositions and association role names, respectively; in so doing, roles permit to give identity to multiple instances of subsystems of the same type, as occurring in redundant configurations (e.g. the power supply in the example).

4.2 DAS Subsystem

DAS hosts a swarm of micro-services consuming information provided by the EIS Knowledge Base to support operation and maintenance processes through a variety of context-dependent techniques.

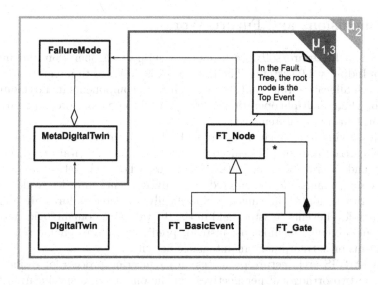

Fig. 4. UML class diagram of the *FT-agent* domain logic as μ_i bounded contexts.

We illustrate the concept with reference to an agent, termed *FT-agent*, which implements Fault Tree Analysis (FTA) [7] so as to enable diagnoses and predictions over system failures [21].

The *FT-agent* is partitioned in 3 micro-services: μ_1 performs analyses over a Fault Tree (FT), combining the outputs provided by the other two micro-services (in the specific project prototype, the task is achieved exploiting the modeling and analysis capabilities offered by the SIRIO Java library included in the ORIS Tool [17], a toolbox for quantitative evaluation of stochastic models); μ_2 exposes a collection of FTs capturing different failure modes of the FS, designed and managed by domain experts and maintenance technicians; μ_3 computes minimal cut-sets and importance measures (e.g. Birnbaum, Fussel-Vesely) over a FT.

Figure 4 represents the domain model of the *FT-agent*, distributed among the three micro-services following the Bounded Context pattern [8]. In the representation, the role of top, basic, or intermediate events in the FT is implemented by an object of type *FailureMode*.

Also in this case, the software architecture promotes an engineering process where models for reliability can be translated into an executable software representation. Specifically, identification of failure modes and their associations with digital twins can be conveniently guided by the artifacts of Failure Mode and Effects Analysis (FMEA) [4]. Additional concepts captured in Failure Mode, Effects, and Criticality Analysis (FMECA), may provide information about criticalities and probabilities, opening the way to the construction of executable quantitative models as data analytics.

5 Conclusions and Future Works

JARVIS is a hardware/software framework supporting operation and maintenance of Industry 4.0 systems. The framework is designed to integrate a System of Systems, allocating roles and responsibilities to components in a dynamic IoT scenario, where multiple operational devices need to be monitored at runtime to enable just-in-time maintenance.

Digital twins have been designed and adopted for representing conceptual composite structures of physical components, offering facilitation to monitor, manage and interact with operating instances, whose telemetries are ingested as IoT data streams and interpreted by analytic agents in order to detect and predict critical failures at runtime. Specifically, detected failures are collected into a high-level events register, held in the digital twins domain logic, and notified to maintenance technicians; instead, predicted failures enable self-healing mechanisms or extraordinary maintenance activities.

The JARVIS architecture promotes an engineering process for resilient systems from two orthogonal perspectives: on the one hand, a specification of the knowledge base of the system is mapped into an executable domain model made of software digital twins; on the other hand, reliability artifacts are translated into runnable failure models. These representations open the way to a variety of runtime monitoring and control services supporting maintainability and resilience.

The project will be completed by mid 2020 with experimentation in a concrete operation scenario, addressing the case of smart city gates for speed control and access regulation to limited traffic zones.

References

1. Abreu, D.P., Velasquez, K., Curado, M., Monteiro, E.: A resilient internet of things architecture for smart cities. Ann. Telecommun. **72**(1–2), 19–30 (2017)
2. Chappell, D.A.: Enterprise Service Bus. O'Reilly Media Inc., Sebastopol (2004)
3. Curry, E.: Message-oriented middleware. In: Middleware for Communications, pp. 1–28 (2004)
4. Department of Defense: MIL-STD-1629A - Procedures for performing a failure mode, effects and criticality analysis. Military Standard, Washington, DC (1980)
5. Di Prospero, A., Norouzi, N., Fokaefs, M., Litoiu, M.: Chatbots as assistants: an architectural framework. In: Proceedings of the 27th Annual International Conference on Computer Science and Software Engineering, pp. 76–86. IBM Corp. (2017)
6. Dragoni, N., et al.: Microservices: yesterday, today, and tomorrow. Present and Ulterior Software Engineering, pp. 195–216. Springer, Cham (2017). https://doi.org/10.1007/978-3-319-67425-4_12
7. Ericson, C.A.: Fault tree analysis. Syst. Saf. Conf. Orlando, Florida **1**, 1–9 (1999)
8. Evans, E.: Domain-Driven Design: Tackling Complexity in the Heart of Software. Addison-Wesley, Boston (2004)

9. Forsberg, K., Mooz, H.: The relationship of system engineering to the project cycle. In: INCOSE International Symposium, vol. 1, pp. 57–65. Wiley Online Library (1991)

10. Friedenthal, S., Moore, A., Steiner, R.: A Practical Guide to SysML: The Systems Modeling Language. Morgan Kaufmann, Burlington (2014)

11. Gamma, E.: Design Patterns: Elements of Reusable Object-Oriented Software. Pearson Education India, New Delhi (1995)

12. Han, J., Haihong, E., Le, G., Du, J.: Survey on NoSQL database. In: 2011 6th International Conference on Pervasive Computing and Applications, pp. 363–366. IEEE (2011)

13. Hohpe, G., Woolf, B.: Enterprise Integration Patterns: Designing, Building, and Deploying Messaging Solutions. Addison-Wesley Professional, Boston (2004)

14. Khan, R., Khan, S.U., Zaheer, R., Khan, S.: Future internet: the internet of things architecture, possible applications and key challenges. In: 2012 10th International Conference on Frontiers of Information Technology, pp. 257–260. IEEE (2012)

15. Linthicum, D.S.: Enterprise Application Integration. Addison-Wesley Professional, Boston (2000)

16. Montesi, F., Weber, J.: Circuit breakers, discovery, and API gateways in microservices. arXiv preprint arXiv:1609.05830 (2016)

17. Paolieri, M., Biagi, M., Carnevali, L., Vicario, E.: The ORIS tool: quantitative evaluation of non-markovian systems. In: IEEE Transactions on Software Engineering (2019)

18. Parri, J., Sampietro, S., Vicario, E.: Deploying digital twins in a lambda architecture for industry 4.0. ERCIM News 115, 30–31 (2018)

19. Pradhan, S., Dubey, A., Gokhale, A.: Designing a resilient deployment and reconfiguration infrastructure for remotely managed cyber-physical systems. In: Crnkovic, I., Troubitsyna, E. (eds.) SERENE 2016. LNCS, vol. 9823, pp. 88–104. Springer, Cham (2016). https://doi.org/10.1007/978-3-319-45892-2_7

20. Radatz, J., Olson, M., Campbell, S.: Mil-std-498. Crosstalk J. Defense Softw. Eng. 8(2), 2–5 (1995)

21. Salfner, F., Lenk, M., Malek, M.: A survey of online failure prediction methods. ACM Comput. Surv. (CSUR) 42(3), 10 (2010)

22. Schmidt, D.C., Stal, M., Rohnert, H., Buschmann, F.: Pattern-Oriented Software Architecture, Patterns for Concurrent and Networked Objects, vol. 2. Wiley, Hoboken (2013)

23. Shrouf, F., Ordieres, J., Miragliotta, G.: Smart factories in industry 4.0: a review of the concept and of energy management approached in production based on the internet of things paradigm. In: 2014 IEEE International Conference on Industrial Engineering and Engineering Management, pp. 697–701. IEEE (2014)

24. Suciu, G., Vulpe, A., Halunga, S., Fratu, O., Todoran, G., Suciu, V.: Smart cities built on resilient cloud computing and secure internet of things. In: 2013 19th international conference on control systems and computer science. pp. 513–518. IEEE (2013)

25. Weippl, E.R., Sanderse, B.: Digital twins - introduction to the special theme. ERCIM News 2018(115), 6–7 (2018)

Testing and Validation Methods

Toward Testing Self-organizations in Multi-Embedded-Agent Systems

Arthur Baudet, Oum-El-Kheir Aktouf$^{(\boxtimes)}$, Annabelle Mercier, and Jean-Paul Jamont

Univ. Grenoble Alpes, Grenoble INP, LCIS, Valence, France
arthur.baudet@grenoble-inp.org,
{oum-el-kheir.aktouf,annabelle.mercier,
jean-paul.jamont}@lcis.grenoble-inp.fr

Abstract. This paper presents a testing approach for validating global adaptation in multi-embedded-agent systems. Those systems are gaining increasing attention due to their high adaptability and resilience. They differ from software multi-agent systems because embedded agents have additional constraints, like energy management that software agents don't. Those constraints and other specificities, like the tight link with the physical environment, require the use of specific methods and tools for testing these systems. The proposed approach aims at validating at run-time the adaptation of those systems when the entities composing them, the agents, are able to change their global behaviors with self-organization processes. Self-organization processes are not specific to multi-agent systems but in their case, they allow agents to change their organization, i.e. their way of interacting, at runtime. The proposed approach and tool are designed to support lifelong monitoring of multi-embedded-agent systems. In such systems, agents have self-organization behaviors resulting in complex and ever adapting systems, which are challenging to test and monitor.

Keywords: Embedded multi-agent systems · Run-time validation · Multi wireless agent communication · Self-organization testing

1 Introduction

To tackle the problem of over increasing complexity, software engineers are using new and innovative ways of thinking, with more distributed data and/or computation. In this context, agent oriented software engineering is gaining increasing attention thanks to some interesting characteristics of multi-agents systems, like high fault-tolerance, flexibility and capacity to adapt to the environment or previous experiences.

There are many definitions of multi-embedded-agent systems (MEAS) or multi-agents systems as they are used in many different scientific fields [14]. From the software engineering point of view [10,13,23] MEAS are seen as systems

© Springer Nature Switzerland AG 2019
R. Calinescu and F. Di Giandomenico (Eds.): SERENE 2019, LNCS 11732, pp. 97–108, 2019.
https://doi.org/10.1007/978-3-030-30856-8_7

revolving around the cooperation of physical autonomous entities called agents. Those agents use cognitive characteristics, like reactivity or proactivity, and cooperation to achieve their goals, known as the local goals. While they are aware of their local goals, agents are not fully aware of the complete system they belong to, and especially the system's goal, known as the global objective. Such systems allow simple or low capability agents to work on simple tasks but achieve, as a whole system, a much more complex objective. A particularity of a multi-agent system, embedded or not, is the absence of a central entity coordinating the agents, so that the system-level decisions are distributed among the agents. The differences due to the embedded feature are related to constraints like energy management, safety management, or other issues related to mobility, communications and integrity of the agents in a physical environment [2]. Those constraints need to be considered in the testing phase. As a consequence, MEAS are not considered as a subpart of multi-agent systems but as a different kind of systems, at least from the testing point of view.

In this context, we are interested in testing the achievement of the global objective, which could be considered as be acceptance testing, from the software engineering perspective. Testing in MEAS is quite challenging because MEAS are asynchronous complex[1] systems of intelligent agents [19]. Very few existing works focus on MEAS, most of them focus only on MAS independently from the implementation of the system under test (SuT). In the following, we will only consider works with hypothesis on the SuT that do not conflict with the constraints added by the embedded feature of MEAS.

Testing the achievement of the global objective is to test if the agents, when working together, produce the expected global output. As there is no central control over the cooperation of the agents, the cooperation is structured by an organization. This organization is known to every agent and is implemented inside the agents. Testing the global objective can then be done by assessing that the organization is correct. In this paper, we will be focusing on the self-organization behaviors. This kind of behavior is the capacity of the agents to create or change the organizations they are in during the execution [5]. It gives the agents the ability to adapt the whole system so it can fit at the best its specifications in a changing environment. Therefore, the organization depends on the agents' autonomy, which increases the difficulty to test it.

Next section introduces challenges of testing self-organization in MEAS. Then a review of existing testing techniques applied to this problem is provided in Sect. 2. In Sect. 3 we provide the adaptation of a MAS testing method to a MEAS through a real life example, and we conclude with main learned aspects and some perspectives for future work in Sect. 4.

2   Review of Testing Methods for Self-organizations

From a testing point of view, MEAS are different from other distributed systems due to the autonomy of the agents. These are intelligent entities which are

---

[1] In the number of variables considered and inter-dependencies between agents.

hard to test [17], mainly due to some cognitive features such as the ability to autonomously make decisions in situations that were not planed. Furthermore, the whole decision process is distributed among them, making the determination and the control of the whole system's behavior very hard, not to say unfeasible.

Self-organizations share those difficulties because the organizations result from the autonomy of the agents. They also add challenges like the error masking. Indeed, errors can be hidden from the tester if the system adapts when agents fail. Not only agents are capable of adapting but the way they globally behave is also adapted, increasing the number of states to consider when testing MEAS [7].

Very few works have been done to test specifically MEAS and even less for testing self-organization in MEAS. In this section we will present the main methods used to test self-organizations in MAS and we'll discuss to what extent they can be applied to MEAS.

2.1 Formal Methods

Formal methods offer systemic ways to check if the self-organization process will work as intended by studying models of the system and its specifications. These methods mainly comprise model-checking, model-based testing and simulation-based testing.

Model checking is one of the most widespread techniques [8,16,20,21]. It consists of modelling the system into a known model and using mathematical tools to prove that the system is correct, based on the model.

Model-based testing methods [15] use modelled specifications to automatically generate test cases with large coverage.

Simulation methods [4,6,18] use modelled system and specifications to run the modelled system through the modelled specifications and analyze results to ensure that the system will behave as expected.

2.2 Run-Time Validation Methods

Run-time validation methods aim to complete the work done at design time assuming that it is really hard to anticipate every external stimuli and mutation of the system. Moreover, they offer tools to help the supervision process through monitoring the system, either by only presenting a more usable view of the system [22] or analyzing the system to highlight possible errors [3,12]. Nevertheless, those systems do not prevent errors from occurring and some work like in [1] try to support the system to prevent it from mutating in wrongful ways.

Generally, formal methods are widely used to guide the developers at design time. However, it is also relevant to add run-time testing to ensure that the system will not misbehave at run-time since MEAS have strong constraints on safety, integrity, and it would require a very complex model to validate those constraints for every possible events during the design phase.

Moreover, automating the validation process at run-time is relevant in our case because we aim at providing a tool for software testers whether they have the mathematical knowledge to use formal methods or not. We do not look for a fully automated system since it will make the testing process complex. Also, we will have to validate the testing approach so keeping it as simple as possible is helping not creating a dependency of complex systems, needing to be able to test another complex system.

3   Testing Multi Wireless Agent Communication

In this section, we develop a run-time system validation method and we show how to apply it to a real life example. To do so, we use the Multi Wireless Agent Communication model (MWAC) described below.

3.1   Definitions

MWAC [11] provides a routing solution for wireless MEAS where no infrastructure for communication exists. Its objective is simple: giving every agent a way to communicate with every other agent. This solution relies on the execution of a routing protocol on a specific organization. This organization is done at run-time via a self-organization mechanism. In our study, we only consider the organization and the self-organization processes.

MWAC defines three roles that can be assigned to the agent. A *representative (r)* manages and routes the messages of nodes that are directly connected to it. To achieve this task, it broadcasts, relays, and responds to route search requests. A *link (l)* enables message exchange between the representative nodes that are directly connected to it. A *simple member (s)* communicates only with the representative node to which it is directly connected. It does not have any routing task to ensure, unless it is the first sender or the final receiver of a message.

Definition 1 (MAS). *Let n be the number of agents, $A_t = (a_i)_{i \in [\![1,n]\!]}$ be the set of agents of the MAS at time $t \in \mathbb{T} \equiv \mathbb{N}$ (the ordered set of dates), a MAS can be modeled as an undirected graph $G_t = (A_t, \omega\_t)$ whose vertices correspond to the agents and the edges represent the connections between agents.*

This graph is called the organizational graph.

Definition 2 (Neighborhood). *Let $t \in \mathbb{T}$ and $a \in A_t$, the neighborhood of a is*

$$V_t(a) = \{a_i \mid i \in [\![1,n]\!], \{a, a_i\} \in \omega\}$$

Remark 1. Suppose $t \in \mathbb{T}$ then $forall\ a_0, a_1 \in A_t$ a_0 adjacent to $a_1 \iff a_0 \in V(a_1) \iff a_1 \in V(a_0)$

Agents determine their roles after analyzing their neighborhood. MWAC uses a specialization of the agents to select the eligible links.

Definition 3 (Role). *Let $\mathcal{R} = \{r, l, s\}$ the set of roles, we define $role : A_t \to \mathcal{R}$ as being the function assigning a role to an agent.*

Definition 4 (Group organization correctness). *The organization inside the groups is considered correct if and only if the following properties are met:*

Let $t \in \mathbb{T}$,
1. $\forall\, a \in A_t\ role(a) = s \iff \exists!\ b \in V(a)\ role(b) = r$

This organization allows the characterization of groups composed by a representative agent together with the agents of its neighborhood. It is worth noting that:

1. each representative agent determines a unique group;
2. each link agent belongs to at least two groups;
3. every simple member belongs to a unique group.

The management of messages is assigned to representative agents that communicate using link agents. An example of this organization is given in Fig. 1.

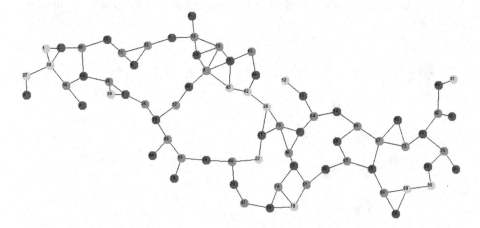

Fig. 1. Simulation of an MEAS executing MWAC. Red = representative, Green = link, Yellow = simple member (Color figure online)

Note 1. When an agent changes role, it broadcasts its new role and groups to its neighborhood.

3.2 Approach Validation

Validation of the self-organization is done in three steps, where each step depends on the validation of the previous one:

1. Stability validation
2. Groups validation
3. Connectivity validation

Stability issues have to be resolved first. The organization can not be fixed just once, it needs to be re-organized, for example to allow agents with low energy level to be replaced. However, the monitoring system should wait for a given time (which depends on the specification) to allow the system to first organize itself or re-organize. This time represents the time given to the system to re-organize. Should it exceed this time, an error will be sent to the operator.

Groups validation is done through the verification of the three properties of Definition 4.

To study connectivity, let's first define an undirected graph $G'_t = (A'_t, \omega')$ at time $t \in \mathbb{T}$ where

$$\forall t \in \mathbb{T} \ A'_t = \{a_i \mid i \in [\![1, n]\!], \ role(a_i) = r\}$$
$$\omega' = \{\{a_i, a_j\} \mid i, j \in [\![1, n]\!], \ \exists a \in A_t, \{a_i, a\}, \{a_j, a\} \in \omega, \ role(a) = l\}$$

The graph represents the groups in the organization. Hence, if the graph is connected, the groups are all connected. If not, there is an error in the organization. An example of organization modelling is given in Fig. 2. This graph is called the *groups graph*.

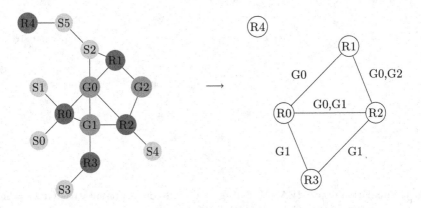

Fig. 2. Example of organization modelling. Red = representative, Green = link, Yellow = simple member (Color figure online)

The Validation Approach. As the SuT is a MEAS, several constraints, mainly due to the embedded dimension, have been considered during the design of the validation approach:

C0: The SuT has a finite amount of energy, so the validation approach must not to put any strains on it.
C1: The SuT is physically distributed, so the validation tool needs to be able to monitor agents on a possibly wide area.
C2: The SuT can have a huge number of agents, so the validation tool needs to be easily scalable.

C0 makes it necessary to only listen to the agent communications and see agents as black boxes. C1 forces the monitoring system to be distributed to cover the SuT. At last, C2 requires the monitoring system to be scalable, since the organization and the group graph can be very large. A solution is to use decentralized computation, the part of the monitoring system will only know a part of the graph and cooperate to validate the whole graph but without one entity knowing the totality of each graph.

The validation approach is therefore a degraded multi-embedded-agent system where the agents are not highly adaptable and where only a fixed plane organization is used. Also, the agents only have basic behavior since they only have to detect errors and not correct them. Each agent knows only a part of the system and may or may not exchange their knowledge to validate the whole system. The cooperation between the testing agents should be minimized; thus lowering the number of messages needed to exchange and so minimizing the impact of the testing system on the SuT.

In the following, we will make the hypothesis that the monitoring system is fully covering the SuT, each agent of the SuT is a neighbor of at least one testing agent.

Stability Validation. To achieve this task, the testing agents do not need to cooperate. Every agent will run the algorithm below.

Algorithm 1. Stability validation

Input: d0, d1 two durations defined from the specifications
```
/* d0 is the maximum duration for one (re-)organization     */
/* d1 is the deadline for the system to be stable           */
```
Output: An error can be detected. The Sut can be considered stable. The Sut graph is constructed

1 **while** *Testing agent is alive* **do**
2   **when** *first organization message is received from sut* **do**
3       $t \longleftarrow$ start_timer()
4   sut_graph $\longleftarrow$ add_message_info()
5   **when** *organization message is received from sut* **do**
6   **if** $t < d0$ **then**
7   sut_graph $\longleftarrow$ add_message_info()
8   **else if** $d0 < t < d1$ **then**
9   trigger_error()
10   **else**
11          $t \longleftarrow$ start_timer()
12   sut_stable $\longleftarrow$ false
13   **when** $t > d0$ **do**
14   sut_stable $\longleftarrow$ true

Groups Validation. As the monitoring system relies on listening the communication inside the SuT, and the MWAC agents do not send their position, the monitoring system can not compute their neighborhood. It could be done by triangulation with the testing agents but this would increase significantly complexity of the monitoring system and generate a huge amount of messages to exchange between the monitoring agents.

Testing the algorithm of group formation needs to be done beforehand.

Connectivity Validation. This task is the most complex one and cooperation between testing agents is necessary. We need to define a distributed decentralized algorithm to determine if the SuT graph is connected when no agent can construct the whole graph (see Algorithm 2).

Note 2. Agent behavior is mostly reactive, so all the algorithms will run simultaneously. Consequently, the **when** statement from different algorithms may refer to the same event.

The main difficulty arises when a validation agent computes two components as being not connected. Indeed, to construct the path between the two components, the validation agent will broadcast a first request and the receiving agents will then broadcast every possible path until a path is created between the two components. This is done by sending a message containing the components and, for each known group not in the received components, if a path exists between one of the agent of the components, a message is broadcast. This message is the start of a possible path. When an agent is able to connect the two components using its knowledge and the knowledge accumulated by the previous agents, it will send a response to the first requester.

As cooperation between agents requires message exchanging, we need to define the messages structure.

Message Structure. The messages are formed as shown in Fig. 3.

message type id	sender id	destination id	message id	sut graph

Fig. 3. Message structure

Where:

message type id indicates the type of the message, see next paragraph from message type description

sender id indicates the id of the *first* agent which sent the message

destination id is most of the time a broadcast id. It is used in the response type message (see next paragraph for message type description)

message id is used to differentiate messages from the same sender

sut graph is the known SuT graph of the sender

Algorithm 2. Connectivity validation

Data: d a duration

```
/* d is maximum duration an agent waits for a response before
   considering that there is no path between its connected
   components and triggering an error                          */
```

Result: An error can be detected, otherwise the organization is considered
valid until the next re-organization

1   **while** *Testing agent is alive* **do**
2   **when** *groups are valid* **do**
3   share_sut_graph_with(neighborhood)

4   **when** *receiving request from neighbor* **do**
5   **if** *is_connected(sut_graph + neighbor_graph)* **then**
6   send_response_to(neighbor, sut_graph)
7   **else**
8   **foreach** *connected agent to neighbor_graph* **do**
9   send_request_to(neighborhood, neighbor_graph + connected agent)

10   **when** *receiving sharing message from neighbor* **do**
11   **if** *not is_connected(sut_graph + neighbor_graph)* **then**
12   send_request_to(neighborhood, sut_graph + neighbor_graph)
13          $t \longleftarrow$ start_timer()

14   **when** *receiving response from neighbor* **do**
15   **if** *response_destination = me and is_connected(sut_graph + response_graph)* **then**
16   add_to_sut_graph(response_graph)
17          $t \longleftarrow 0$
18   **else**
19   send_response_to(response_destination, response_graph)

20   **when** $t > d$ **do**
21   trigger_error()

Message Types. There are four message types:

sharing is used to first share the SuT graph with the agent neighborhood, resulting in overlapping graphs which are easier to test.

request is used when the SuT graph of an agent is not connected, it will broadcast a request waiting for an other agent to respond with a path between its connected sub-graphs. The **sender id** is never changed. To know to which an agent should respond, it will have to keep the couple **sender id**, **message id** linked with the id of the agent which really sent the message.

response is used to respond to a request. The **destination id** must correspond to the requester's id so the response can be forwarded back to it.

wait is used to help the agents synchronize. Every agents may not reach the third step at the same time, the **wait** message is used when a request is sent to an agent in the first two steps. It will tell the requester to wait a response without starting the timer and put the requester in waiting mode. An agent in waiting mode receiving a request to which it does not know the response will also send a `wait` message. This does not create deadlock since even if an agent never reaches the third step it will itself eventually timeout.

Note 3. To avoid the count to infinity problem [9], every received graph will be linked with the agent sending them.

Experimentation and Results. As first results, we were able to detect a known error in the MWAC self-organization process: as it can be seen in the Fig. 1, the group of agents 3 and 37 (left of the picture) is not connected to the other groups. This error can happen when the density of agents is low. With a hexagonal covering of the SuT shown in Fig. 4 we could detect this error in several layouts and with a population ranging from low population with a layout inclined to make the error occur to randomized layouts of population up to hundreds of tested agents.

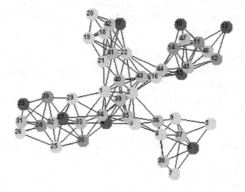

Fig. 4. Example of use of our approach. Red = representative, Green = link, Yellow = simple member, Cyan = validation agent (Color figure online)

From all tested layouts, we detected the known error but there were also false positives when the path between components observed as disconnected could not be found by the validation system even if it existed. This is due to the solution used to reduce the number of broadcast messages. When the layout and the self-organization algorithm lead to components with very few and long paths between them, the computation of those paths may be impaired by the solution used to prevent broadcast tempests, leading to the detection of an error when there is none.

A solution to this problem would be to add some routing capabilities to the validation agents to reduce the number of broadcast messages and enhance the path finding between components.

4   Conclusion and Future Work

We motivated the need of specific methods to test self-organizations in embedded multi-agent systems and highlighted the differences between MEAS and software MAS. After a presentation of methods that could be adapted to embedded multi-agents, we proposed applying run-time monitoring to validate organization as they are changed by the agents. Last, we presented a case study to apply this method, the associated challenges and some encouraging results.

Future Work includes working on the distributed algorithm computing whether or not the routing graph is connected, thoroughly validate the testing approach with different varieties of layouts and high population SuT. Finally, we are aiming to apply this approach to other similar MEAS.

References

1. Abbass, H.A., Harvey, J., Yaxley, K.: Lifelong testing of smart autonomous systems by shepherding a swarm of watchdog artificial intelligence agents. CoRR abs/1812.08960 (2018)
2. Barnier, C., Aktouf, O., Mercier, A., Jamont, J.: Toward an embedded multi-agent system methodology and positioning on testing. In: 2017 IEEE International Symposium on Software Reliability Engineering Workshops (ISSREW) (2017). https://doi.org/10.1109/ISSREW.2017.57
3. Bulling, N., Dastani, M., Knobbout, M.: Monitoring norm violations in multi-agent systems. In: Proceedings of the 2013 International Conference on Autonomous Agents and Multi-Agent Systems (2013)
4. De Wolf, T., Holvoet, T., Samaey, G.: Engineering self-organising emergent systems with simulation-based scientific analysis. In: Proceedings of the Fourth International Workshop on Engineering Self-Organising Applications (2005)
5. Di Marzo Serugendo, G., Gleizes, M.P., Karageorgos, A.: Self-organization in multi-agent systems. Knowl. Eng. Rev. **20**, (2005). https://doi.org/10.1017/S0269888905000494
6. Dikenelli, O., Gürcan, Ö., Çakırlar, I., Bora, Ş.: Ratkit: a repeatable automated testing toolkit for agent-based modeling and simulation. In: The 15th International Workshop on Multi-Agent Simulation (MABS 2014), 13th International Conference on Autonomous Agents and Multiagent Systems (AAMAS 2014) (2014)
7. Eberhardinger, B., Anders, G., Seebach, H., Siefert, F., Knapp, A., Reif, W.: An approach for isolated testing of self-organization algorithms. In: de Lemos, R., Garlan, D., Ghezzi, C., Giese, H. (eds.) Software Engineering for Self-Adaptive Systems III. Assurances. LNCS, vol. 9640, pp. 188–222. Springer, Cham (2017). https://doi.org/10.1007/978-3-319-74183-3_7
8. El Fallah-Seghrouchni, A., Degirmenciyan Cartault, I., Marc, F.: Modelling, control and validation of multi-agent plans in dynamic context. In: Proceedings of the Third International Joint Conference on Autonomous Agents and Multiagent Systems - Volume 1 (2004). https://doi.org/10.1109/AAMAS.2004.175
9. Elmeleegy, K., Cox, A.L., Ng, T.S.E.: Understanding and mitigating the effects of count to infinity in ethernet networks. IEEE/ACM Trans. Netw. **17** (2009). https://doi.org/10.1109/TNET.2008.920874

10. Greenberg, M.S., Byington, J.C., Harper, D.G.: Mobile agents and security. IEEE Commun. Mag. **36** (1998). https://doi.org/10.1109/35.689634
11. Hamani, N., Jamont, J., Occello, M., Ben-Yelles, C., Lagreze, A., Koudil, M.: A multi-cooperative-based approach to manage communication in wireless instrumentation systems. IEEE Syst. J. **12**, (2018). https://doi.org/10.1109/JSYST. 2017.2721220
12. Helsinger, A., Lazarus, R., Wright, W., Zinky, J.: Tools and techniques for performance measurement of large distributed multiagent systems. In: Proceedings of the Second International Joint Conference on Autonomous Agents and Multiagent Systems (2003). https://doi.org/10.1145/860575.860711
13. Huhns, M.N., Stephens, L.M.: Multiagent systems and societies of agents. Multiagent Syst. Mod. Approach Distrib. Artif. Intell. **1**, 79–114 (1999)
14. Jamont, J., Occello, M.: Meeting the challenges of decentralised embedded applications using multi-agent systems. IJAOSE **5**(1), 22–68 (2015). https://doi.org/ 10.1504/IJAOSE.2015.078435
15. Kerraoui, S., Kissoum, Y., Redjimi, M., Saker, M.: MATT: multi agents testing tool based nets within nets. J. Inf. Organ. Sci. **40** (2016). https://doi.org/10.31341/ jios.40.2.1
16. Lomuscio, A., Qu, H., Raimondi, F.: MCMAS: an open-source model checker for theverification of multi-agent systems. Int. J. Softw. Tools Technol. Transfer **19** (2017). https://doi.org/10.1007/s10009-015-0378-x
17. Meziane, F., Vadera, S.: Artificial Intelligence Applications for Improved Software Engineering Development: New Prospects. IGI Global, Hershey (2009)
18. Niazi, M.A., Hussain, A., Kolberg, M.: Verification & validation of agent based simulations using the VOMAS (virtual overlay multi-agent system) approach. CoRR abs/1708.02361 (2017)
19. Rouff, C.: A test agent for testing agents and their communities. In: Proceedings, IEEE Aerospace Conference, vol. 5 (2002). https://doi.org/10.1109/AERO.2002. 1035446
20. Rouff, C., Buskens, R., Pullum, L., Cui, X., Hinchey, M.: The adaptiv approach to verification of adaptive systems. In: Proceedings of the Fifth International C* Conference on Computer Science and Software Engineering (2012). https://doi. org/10.1145/2347583.2347600
21. Samaey, G., Holvoet, T., Wolf, T.D.: Using equation-free macroscopic analysis for studying self-organising emergent solutions. In: 2008 Second IEEE International Conference on Self-Adaptive and Self-Organizing Systems (2008). https://doi.org/ 10.1109/SASO.2008.30
22. Tonn, J., Kaiser, S.: ASGARD - a graphical monitoring tool for distributed agent infrastructures. In: Demazeau, Y., Dignum, F., Corchado, J.M., Pérez, J.B. (eds.) Advances in Practical Applications of Agents and Multiagent Systems. AINSC, vol. 70. Springer, Berlin (2010). https://doi.org/10.1007/978-3-642-12384-9_21
23. Wooldridge, M., Jennings, N.R.: Intelligent agents: theory and practice. Knowl. Eng. Rev. **10** (1995). https://doi.org/10.1017/S0269888900008122

Towards Integrated Correctness Analysis and Performance Evaluation of Software Systems (Doctoral Forum Paper)

Ioannis Stefanakos[(✉)]

Department of Computer Science, University of York, York, UK
is742@york.ac.uk

Abstract. In recent times, the involvement of computer systems in our lives has been drastically increasing, as has the need of improving the resilience of these systems, e.g. so they can withstand errors and changes in their environment. Techniques such as testing and simulation are often used to ensure this, but in the case of complex, real-time systems, these techniques can only provide coverage for a limited set of possible system behaviours. Software model checking and stochastic verification are alternative techniques that formally and exhaustively verify whether software meets its functional requirements and establish the performance and dependability properties of software, respectively. The two formal techniques are often used in isolation, yet software must simultaneously ensure a combination of functional and non-functional requirements. The doctoral project described in this paper aims to bring these two areas of software verification together by enabling the joint analysis of functional and non-functional properties of software systems.

1 Introduction

It has long been known that computer systems, both hardware and software, exhibit errors. In order to increase the reliability of these systems, software engineers may devote a substantial amount of time on testing and debugging. There has always been research focusing on developing new or improving the existing verification methods [1]. Verification is the area that includes all the techniques aiming to improve software quality and its main focus is to provide evidence that the final product conforms to the specified requirements during all of its life cycle processes [2]. Some of the techniques subsumed under verification are formal verification, testing and simulation.

Testing is considered an essential activity in software engineering. It is defined as the process of validation of the system's intended behaviour and identification of potential malfunctions [3]. With the increase of involvement of software and hardware systems in our everyday lives, testing has become more complex but at the same time necessary to ensure the correct functionality of these systems.

Work supported by Microsoft Research through its PhD Scholarship Programme.

R. Calinescu and F. Di Giandomenico (Eds.): SERENE 2019, LNCS 11732, pp. 109–117, 2019.
https://doi.org/10.1007/978-3-030-30856-8_8

Although successful testing identifies a significant amount of errors, it is still impossible to capture all of them [4], especially in dynamic environments. As a result, computer systems can still be afflicted by errors which could potentially lead to severe consequences, e.g. safety critical systems.

Stochastic verification and model checking are techniques able to address issues that testing is not able to identify. Both of these techniques are also known as formal methods, which is a line of study that depends on the fact that computer systems can be depicted as mathematical objects whose behaviour is in principle well-determined [1].

Model checking provides an automated method for verifying concurrent finite-state systems in which the system's intended behaviour is represented by a state-graph model checked to confirm it satisfies properties formalized in temporal logic [5]. The system semantics are given by means of a Kripke structure and the specification is expressed using temporal logic. Temporal logic is a formalism for reasoning about time without introducing it explicitly [6].

A Kripke structure (KS) is a labeled graph that contains all the possible states of a system and the transitions between them. The states are represented by the vertices of the graph and the transitions by its edges. In more detail, a tuple $M = (S, S_0, R, AP, L)$ is the representation of a Kripke structure where S is a set of states, $S_0 \subseteq S$ is a set of the initial states, $R \subseteq S \times S$ is a transition relation, AP is a set of atomic propositions and $L : S \rightarrow 2^{AP}$ is a labeling function that maps each state to the set of propositional variables that hold in it [7]. The states represent the different states of a system. The main difference between Kripke structures and labelled transition systems (LTS), which is another popular basis for many formal modelling languages, is that transitions in LTS are labelled to describe the actions which cause a state change while the states in KS are labelled to describe how they are modified by the transitions [8].

Stochastic verification (also known as probabilistic model checking) is a formal verification method that can establish quality properties of software systems that exhibit stochastic behaviour [9]. Software systems of this nature can be found in applications used in aircrafts and vehicles, as well as in personal devices such as mobile phones. In order to be able to verify the correctness of the systems operating under uncertain environments, it is necessary to analyze quantitative properties such as performance and reliability.

Probabilistic model checking uses models that can be categorized as continuous and discrete time, deterministic and non-deterministic, and compositional. The simplest type of all probabilistic models is the Discrete-Time Markov Chains (DTMCs) [10]. DTMCs are Kripke structures that all their transitions are linked to a specific probability. The sum of all out-going transition probabilities, that each state has, is equal to one.

Model checking and probabilistic model checking are necessary to ensure that the produced software meets both functional and non-functional requirements. While their importance is recognized, software engineers often only consider one or the other during their software analysis and this has mainly to do with the

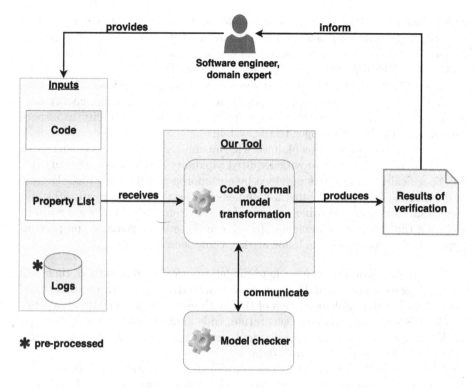

Fig. 1. High-level diagram of the proposed approach

fact that these techniques use disjoint models, different formalisms, etc. This project aims to bring together the two areas of verification by (a) extending existing modelling paradigms in order to integrate the verification of both functional and non-functional requirements, and (b) achieving this integration with an acceptable cost and good scalability that enables the application of the new verification techniques to real-world systems.

2   Objectives and Proposed Solution

The project focuses on constructing state-transition models (e.g., Kripke structures and discrete-time Markov chains or DTMCs [10]) of the source code under verification, through the implementation of a code-to-model transformation method. This method will be implemented as a hybrid verification tool. Additionally, a list of properties to be verified will be given as input to the tool. To enable the analysis of non-functional properties, the tool will also use as input preprocessed logs of the system. These logs will capture the operational profile of the software, and will be used to calculate the probability of executing different branches within the code, based on previous use. The resulting probabilities will be assigned to the respective state transitions of the generated DTMC model which, finally, together with the source code will be analyzed by model checkers, to verify both functional and non-functional properties of interest. When fully developed, the approach may use model checkers and verification tools such as Storm [11], NuSMV [12], Java PathFinder (JPF) [13], FACT [14,15], ePMC [16] and OMNI [17,18]. The joint analysis of functional (e.g. deadlock freeness, reachability) and non-functional requirements (e.g. response time, energy consumption) will provide insight to software engineers and the ability to inspect the impact of different changes to the system.

Moreover, our project was planned with an emphasis on resilience, which can be defined as the ability to provide required capability in the face of adversity [19, 20]. Specifically, the analysis provided by our approach will enable the selection, at design time or runtime, of method implementations (code) that can withstand the actual workload and other aspects of the environment of a system without violating the system requirements. To achieve the project goals, we propose an approach that comprises the following key components:

- The implementation of a code-to-model transformation method that will enable the conversion of Java source code into Kripke structures and DTMC models. For the implementation of this method, we used JavaParser[1], a set of libraries that supports code generation, code analysis and code refactoring.
- A list of input parameters for our tool, i.e. source code, properties of interest and pre-processed logs of user data.
- A communication channel between our tool and popular model checkers, some of them mentioned earlier, for the verification of both functional and non-functional requirements.

Figure 1 depicts the high-level architecture of our solution. In the first step, the software engineer/domain expert will submit the required inputs to our tool. In the next step, the tool will generate the formal models based on the input data, and will communicate with the model checkers to initiate the verification procedure. As soon as this process finishes, the tool will receive the results and will produce an output file, which can be used by the engineer to detect requirement violations.

To achieve the project objectives, we have organized the research work into the following tasks:

1. Review existing literature on joint verification of functional and non-functional requirements to learn the current state of research. The outcome of this literature review is summarized in Sect. 4.
2. Based on the identified limitations, form a theoretical method as a potential solution. A first version of this solution was described earlier in this section.
3. Proceed with the implementation of the proposed theoretical method. The preliminary implementation work carried out so far is presented in Sect. 3.
4. Evaluate the method using case studies taken from model checking benchmarks and real-world applications (e.g. Android code).

---

[1] https://javaparser.org.

```
X.java                                    1  dtmc
  1  class X {                             2
  2⊖     void x(int i) {                   3  const double p1;
  3         if (i>3) {                     4  const double p2;
  4             i=5;                        5  const double p3;
  5         }                               6
  6         else {                          7  module method_X
  7             if (i>1) {                  8
  8                 i=5;                    9    s : [0..7] init 1;
  9             }                          10
 10             else {                     11    [] s=0 -> p1:(s'=1) + (1-p1):(s'=2); //line 3
 11                 i=1;                    12    [] s=1 -> 1:(s'=5);                 //line 4
 12             }                          13    [] s=2 -> p2:(s'=3) + (1-p2):(s'=4); //line 7
 13         }                              14    [] s=3 -> 1:(s'=5);                 //line 8
 14         if (i==1) {                    15    [] s=4 -> 1:(s'=5);                 //line 11
 15             i++;                       16    [] s=5 -> p3:(s'=6) + (1-p3):(s'=7); //line 14
 16         }                              17    [] s=6 -> 1:(s'=7);                 //line 15
 17     }                                  18    [] s=7 -> true;                     //end of program
 18  }                                     19
 19                                        20  endmodule
 20                                        21
 21                                        22
                                           23  |
                                           24
                                    Model  Properties  Simulator  Log
```

Fig. 2. Example of input source code (left) and output DTMC model (right)

5. Extend the approach to support further automation of the method and apply additional techniques (e.g. parametric model checking).
6. Further evaluate and refine our framework, making any necessary improvements based on the evaluation results.

3 Preliminary Work

So far, the project has developed a preliminary version of the approach from Fig. 1. This version of our verification tool supports only the transformation of Java source code into a DTMC model. Thus, the verification process is currently performed manually, using the probabilistic model checker PRISM (www. prismmodelchecker.org) after the automated generation of the DTMC.

Figure 2 presents an example of the tool's input and output. At this stage, the tool is only able to extract a DTMC model from a given source code (with transition probabilities represented as parameters of the DTMC model). We still need the logs of user data to reason about them, which is one of the future steps of the project, along with the choice of appropriate model checkers (some mentioned earlier) to complete the verification process.

Focusing on this example, every variable assignment in the code is represented by a new state in the DTMC model and can lead to a another state with probability $P = 1$. The if statements on the other hand, also represented by a new state in the model, lead to two possible states. One with probability P if the condition is satisfied and a second one with probability $1 - P$, in the case the condition is not satisfied. In the latter case, we move to the else branch, if it exists, or to the next expression. For instance, consider the if statement starting in line 3 of the Java code from Fig. 2; the if branch of this conditional statement is executed for $i > 3$. Therefore, if the log of an application that uses this code shows that i is equally likely to take the values $0, 1, \ldots, 9$, the probability that the if branch is executed will be 0.7, and the probability that the else branch is executed will be 0.3. Of course, in real systems, the conditions are often more complex, and the values of variables are rarely uniformly distributed like in this simple example.

The method shows some promising preliminary results. In preliminary testing, we allocated a time counter under specific branches of the source code and then performed simulation to calculate the average response time. Next, we added reward structures in the DTMC model (e.g. *rewards "execTime"* $s = 1 : 2$; $s = 3 : 1$; *endrewards*), to assign the corresponding states with the same time values used in the source code. To deal with probabilities at this stage, we created a uniform distribution of values ranging between -1 and 1. The final results derived from the model were finally obtained by establishing and verifying properties in Probabilistic Computation Tree Logic (PCTL) [21], e.g. $R \ \{ \text{"execTime"} \} =? \ [F \ s \ = \ 7]$. This property specification translates to what is the total execution time by the time we reach program termination. The simulation and probabilistic model checking produced the same results in these preliminary experiments.

4   Related Work

While several studies have been conducted in the areas of model checking and probabilistic model checking, with notable advances in both [6,9,22,23], there are significantly fewer approaches when it comes to combining these two techniques.

Cortellessa et al. [24] build an XML-based framework that consists of software models and formal relations among them, to support the integration of functional and non-functional analysis of software systems. The XML representation is translated by an Analysis filter as input of the desired analysis methodology. The two considered methodologies are CHARMY and TwoTowers. The former specifies software architectures and their behavioural properties by using state machines and scenarios as the source notation. Model checking is then performed to these notations in order to evaluate the consistency between the software architecture and the functional requirements. The latter supports the validation of performance requirements at an architectural level. It takes as input an AEmilia textual description (ADL), builds the corresponding Markov model and evaluates the performance indices of interest. Feedback is then provided whether the model should be modified. Despite the joint functional and non-functional analysis, this work is limited at architectural level and to the integration of only two methodologies.

Nostro et al. [25] present an approach for the automated synthesis of application layer connectors between heterogeneous networked systems, addressing functional and non-functional interoperability that takes place both at pre-deployment and run-time. During pre-deployment time, an analysis module receives the applications' specifications and through their analysis, synthesizes a mediator that enables the functional inter-operation among them. Following, a connector analysis module takes as input the synthesized mediator and the non-functional requirements and performs a stochastic model-based analysis to evaluate the desired non-functional properties. Feedback is provided back to the connector synthesis module about the system's expected operation and how to improve the synthesized mediator in the case that the non-functional requirements are not met. Pre-deployment time's output is a connector that satisfies both functional and non-functional requirements. At run-time, probes are used on the applications and the synthesized mediator to monitor the connected system. When a violation occurs, the probes identify it and trigger the adaptation process, re-evaluating the new specification. Similarly to the previous approach, this one is limited at architectural level and needs to address open issues such as analysis optimization and scalability aspects.

Filieri et al. [26,27] introduce a general methodology that uses symbolic execution of source code for extracting failure and success paths that can be used for probabilistic reliability assessment. The result of symbolic execution is a finite set of paths, each with a path condition. These paths can either lead to success, failure or can be interrupted by the bounded exploration. These approaches perform reliability analysis directly on source code, in contrast with most of the current approaches that are limited on architectural level. However, only reliability has been addressed, and the bounded exploration can potentially lead to loss of information necessary for non-functional property analysis. Our research aims to address the problem of bounded exploration of loops, and to consider additional non-functional properties, e.g. performance.

5   Conclusion

Model checking and probabilistic model checking are techniques widely used to verify functional properties of software systems and to establishing performance and dependability properties of these systems, respectively. However, the two techniques are often used in isolation. Their integration is difficult due to the different formalisms and models they use. Additionally, most of the current approaches are limited at architectural level, and the ones focused on source code have limitations in both exploration depth and variety of non-functional properties. In this doctoral paper, we proposed an approach that combines the two techniques at source code level, with the aim to provide insight to software engineers about violations of functional and non-functional requirements of software systems.

References

1. Emerson, E.A.: The beginning of model checking: a personal perspective. In: 18th International Conference on Computer Aided Verification, pp. 27–45 (2008)

2. IEEE Standard for System and Software Verification and Validation. In: IEEE Std 1012–2012, pp. 1–223 (2012)
3. Bertolino, A.: Software testing research: achievements, challenges, dreams. In: FOSE 2007, pp. 85–103 (2007)
4. Lee, P., Verma, S., Harris, I.G.: A Comparison of Error Detection between Simulation-based Validation and Model Checking. University of California, Center for Embedded Computer Systems (2013)
5. Alur, R., Courcoubetis, C., Dill, D.: Model-checking for real-time systems. In: LICS 1990, pp. 414–425 (1990)
6. Clarke, E.M., Lerda, F.: Model Checking: Software and Beyond. J. Universal Computer Science 13, 639–649 (2007)
7. Clarke, E.M.: The birth of model checking. In: Grumberg, O., Veith, H. (eds.) 25 Years of Model Checking. LNCS, vol. 5000, pp. 1–26. Springer, Heidelberg (2008). https://doi.org/10.1007/978-3-540-69850-0_1
8. De Nicola, R., Vaandrager, F.: Action versus state based logics for transition systems. In: Guessarian, I. (ed.), Semantics of Systems of Concurrent Processes, pp. 407–419 (1990)
9. Kwiatkowska, M., Norman, G., Parker, D.: Advances and challenges of probabilistic model checking. In: Allerton 2010, pp. 1691–1698 (2010)
10. Norman, G., Parker, D., Kwiatkowska, M., et al.: Using probabilistic model checking for dynamic power management. Formal Aspects Comput. 17(2), 160–176 (2005)
11. Dehnert, C., Junges, S., Katoen, J.-P., Volk, M.: A storm is coming: a modern probabilistic model checker. In: CAV 2017, pp. 592–600, (2017)
12. Cimatti, A., et al.: NuSMV 2: an opensource tool for symbolic model checking. In: Brinksma, E., Larsen, K.G. (eds.) CAV 2002. LNCS, vol. 2404, pp. 359–364. Springer, Heidelberg (2002). https://doi.org/10.1007/3-540-45657-0_29
13. Brat, G., Havelund, K., Park, S., Visser, W.: Java PathFinder - second generation of a Java model checker, Advances in Verification Workshop (2000)
14. Calinescu, R., Ghezzi, C., Johnson, K., Pezzè, M., Rafiq, Y., Tamburrelli, G.: Formal verification with confidence intervals to establish quality of service properties of software systems. IEEE Transact. Reliab. 65(1), 107–125 (2015)
15. Calinescu, R., Johnson, K., Paterson, C.: FACT: a probabilistic model checker for formal verification with confidence intervals. In: Chechik, M., Raskin, J.-F. (eds.) TACAS 2016. LNCS, vol. 9636, pp. 540–546. Springer, Heidelberg (2016). https://doi.org/10.1007/978-3-662-49674-9_32
16. Calinescu, R., Paterson, C.A., Johnson, K.: Efficient parametric model checking using domain knowledge. In: IEEE Transactions on Software Engineering (2018). https://doi.org/10.1109/TSE.2019.2912958
17. Paterson, C.A., Calinescu, R.: Accurate analysis of quality properties of software with observation-based Markov chain refinement. In: ICSA 2017, pp. 121–130 (2017)
18. Paterson, C.A., Calinescu, R.: Observation-enhanced QoS analysis of component-based systems. In: IEEE Transactions on Software Engineering (2018). https://doi.org/10.1109/TSE.2018.2864159
19. INCOSE, Resilient Systems Homepage. https://www.incose.org/incose-member-resources/working-groups/analytic/resilient-systems. Accessed 11 June 2019
20. Bennaceur, A., et al.: Modelling and analysing resilient cyber-physical systems. In: SEAMS SEAMS 2019, pp. 70–76 (2019)
21. Hansson, H., Jonsson, B.: A logic for reasoning about time and reliability. Formal Aspects Comput. 6(5), 512–535 (1994)

22. Calinescu, R., Kikuchi, S.: Formal methods @ runtime. In: Calinescu, R., Jackson, E. (eds.) Monterey Workshop 2010. LNCS, vol. 6662, pp. 122–135. Springer, Heidelberg (2011). https://doi.org/10.1007/978-3-642-21292-5_7
23. Calinescu, R., et al.: Synthesis and verification of self-aware computing systems. Self-Aware Computing Systems, pp. 337–373. Springer, Cham (2017). https://doi.org/10.1007/978-3-319-47474-8_11
24. Cortellessa, V., et al.: A framework for the integration of functional and non-functional analysis of software architectures. Electron. Notes Theoret. Comput. Sci. **116**, 31–44 (2005)
25. Nostro, N., et al.: Achieving functional and non functional interoperability through synthesized connectors. J. Syst. Softw. **111**, 185–199 (2016)
26. Filieri, A., Pasareanu, C.S., Yang, G.: Quantification of software changes through probabilistic symbolic execution. In: ASE 2015, pp. 703–708 (2016)
27. Filieri, A., Pasareanu, C.S., Visser, W.: Reliability analysis in symbolic pathfinder. In: ICSE 2013, pp. 622–631 (2013)

Security, Trust and Privacy Management

An Energy Aware Approach to Trust Management Systems for Embedded Multi-Agent Systems

Arthur Darroux, Jean-Paul Jamont, Oum-El-Kheir Aktouf[✉],
and Annabelle Mercier

Univ. Grenoble Alpes, Grenoble INP, LCIS, Valence, France
arthur.darroux@grenoble-inp.org, {jean-paul.jamont,oum-el-kheir.aktouf,
annabelle.mercier}@lcis.grenoble-inp.fr

Abstract. With the growing interest toward pervasive systems such as the Internet of Things or Cyber-Physical Systems, embedded multi-agent systems have been increasingly investigated. In these systems, agents cooperate to achieve their local goals and a global goal that would be impossible for an isolated agent to achieve. However, the dark side of this collaboration is that agents can easily be victim of malicious attacks coming from untrustworthy agents. Consequently, trust management systems are designed to help agents choosing trustworthy counterparts to cooperate based on available information. But gathering the necessary information may be too expensive in terms of energy for small embedded agents and not relevant in all contexts. We propose a solution that allows agents to manage the energy consumption associated with information gathering. Our solution uses a Multi-Armed Bandit algorithm, which is a reinforcement learning technique to allow the agents to adapt themselves and their energy consumption to the context.

Keywords: Embedded multi-agent systems · Security ·
Trust management · Energy awareness · Multi-armed bandit

1 Introduction

Agent-Oriented Software Engineering (AOSE) aims at developing distributed and decentralised systems where entities (called agents) autonomously interact with each others. Agents only have a local view of their environment and other agents of the system. Thus, in order to fulfil the goal of the system, agents have to work in collaboration. Agents can make decisions in situations that weren't planed and without the help of an operator (decision autonomy). Agents are also flexible, meaning that their decisions are based on what they perceive of their environment (reactivity), their goals (proactivity) and their relationships with other agents (social ability) [10]. Multi-agent systems (MAS) are used in e-business contexts but also in ad-hoc networks, Internet of Things (IoT) and Cyber-Physical Systems (CPSs).

© Springer Nature Switzerland AG 2019
R. Calinescu and F. Di Giandomenico (Eds.): SERENE 2019, LNCS 11732, pp. 121–137, 2019.
https://doi.org/10.1007/978-3-030-30856-8_9

This paper focuses on Embedded Multi-Agents Systems (EMAS [8]). We define an EMAS as a MAS that includes (but is not restricted to) agents that can interact with the physical world (through sensors and actuators). Examples of these systems are wireless sensor networks, IoT systems, Vehicular Ad Hoc Networks (VANET), etc.

EMAS are also often open and heterogeneous systems. *Heterogeneity* is the fact that all agents don't have the same features (in terms of computational power, energy constraints, etc.). This is often the case in EMAS since embedded agents often interact with software agents running on computers with much more computational power. The *openness* of the systems is the allowance to agents to enter and leave the system dynamically [21]. Many EMAS are open systems because of the nature of agents that work at a local scale and the wireless nature of communications that are widely used in this domain, allowing new agents to interact with agents from the system at any time.

Security has become a major concern in computing systems in general, especially open ones such as multi-agent systems. To ensure confidentiality, integrity, availability, systems have to use secure communications and protect agents from software and hardware attacks. In a multi-agent context, a drawback of relying on a collective activity for a global task is that it increases the system vulnerability to failures or malicious behaviours. If an agent does not behave as expected, it will influence the outcome of the system's global task. The autonomous nature of agents and the necessity to cooperate with other agents bring some new challenges. Agents have to autonomously choose other agents to interact with. To ensure the system's security, decisions made by agents need to be reliable. This means that trustworthy agents shouldn't interact with agents that aim at breaking the system [16] (e.g. by disclosing private information, or refusing to cooperate in a Denial of Service fashion.). In EMAS, this concern is reinforced because not only malicious agents can enter the system because of its openness, but also trustworthy agents can be corrupted. Indeed, corrupting agents can be performed easily since embedded agents have (most of the time) low capabilities and can be victim of software and hardware attacks. To tackle multi-agent systems' security issues, the concept of trust has been introduced and widely studied in the literature. The rational from this concept is to help the agent's decision making process by making the agents choose other trustworthy agents to interact with.

In this paper, we propose a lightweight trust model to help agents to manage their energy consumption due to the trust management process. We use Multi-Armed Bandit (MAB) learning algorithms to enable an agent to select trustworthy neighbouring agents with whom to cooperate. The main originality of our model is that it takes into account the energy cost of calculating trust related values, thus helping each agent to answer the question: is it worth it to spend energy to have better values of trust or not?

This paper is organised as follows. Section 2 introduces the general background of this work by further describing the concept of trust and its related features (information sources, models and constraints). Section 3 describes the proposed energy management process within a lightweight trust management system by using a Multi-Armed Bandit learning based approach. As far as we know, this is an original approach for making trust management system energy-aware. A case study is also introduced. Section 4 concludes this paper and summarises future research directions.

2 Trust Management Systems for Embedded Multi-Agent Systems

In this section, we first provide an overview the trust notion. Then, we analyze existing trust management systems (TMS) in an EMAS context, following four main features: (Sect. 2.2) information sources (Sect. 2.3) models of trust within an agent (Sect. 2.4) vulnerability of TMS, and (Sect. 2.5) constraints, related to limited resources in EMAS.

2.1 Security and Trust

Trust is a concept that we can intuitively understand but is hard to define [5]. Nevertheless, the benefits of its application in computing and distributed systems is widely agreed. Many works have been done to use it in distributed systems and many TMS have been designed to help agents make a better decision [7,15,16,19,22,23,29,30].

Due to the large interest given to TMS, very different approaches can be found in the literature. The first major difference between existing approaches comes from the presence or not of a central trusted entity that is in charge of managing trust in the system. Systems where such an entity exists are called centralised while the other ones other ones are called distributed or decentralised. The second main difference comes from the fact that trust associated to an agent can be global and shared by all agents, or subjective to each agent.

Furthermore, as stated by [19] TMS can be split into three main components: *trust management, trust modelling* and *decision making* (see Fig. 1). Trust management describes how evidences are gathered from past interactions, contexts and other agents. Trust modelling is the computational model used to represent trust in an agent. It describes how trust related values are represented (as binary values trusted or not trusted or as multi-dimensional continuous values representing different values of trust in different contexts) and how they are calculated from evidences (using a probabilistic approach, or fuzzy logic). Decision making describes how decisions are made based on trust values.

Since agents in EMAS only have a partial view of other members of the system, they will not always be able to communicate with other agents; so we cannot rely on a central trusted entity to manage the trust calculation and decision making. Besides, using a central entity will cause some scalability issues in the system and contradict the distributed nature of multi-agent systems. Consequently, our work is based on decentralised and subjective TMS. This means that agents have to evaluate their possible partners themselves. This condition implies some constraint on the trust management systems: TMS shouldn't be too resource consuming for embedded agents with low computational power and energy limitation [24,30].

Fig. 1. Trust management system

2.2 Information Sources

Most information used to build trust with a system is related to past experiences of the system. However, additional information can be considered. Three main types of information can be distinguished according to their respective sources:

- Direct information: information that an agent can acquire by itself (self-acquired) [22,23,27,29,30]. Direct information is the most reliable and used one. However, it is the less available one, especially in open systems. Two main types of direct information have been distinguished [23]: information issued from direct experience of an agent, and information observed by an agent from interactions between other agents.
- Indirect information: this type of information is still based on interactions between agents. However, it is not directly observed as in the first case, but it is transmitted to the agent by other intermediate agents. This type of information is usually called "recommendation". Trust models based on indirect information are called reputation models [23]. This type of information is more available than the preceding one, however it can be issued by malicious agents.
- Socio-cognitive information: this type of information is derived from intrinsic features of the agents [29].

2.3 Models

Trust models help in figuring out how trust is represented within an agent [22]. Two ways of classifying a trust model are:

- The trust scale: this may correspond to discrete or continuous values.
- The trust dimension: refers to the number of values associated to the trust. Different values may be used to represent trust if different contexts.

[18] stresses the fact that both categories above are closely related to the associated semantics.

2.4   Vulnerability

As a security feature, a TMS may be prone to some weaknesses that allow attackers to avoid protection provided by the TMS. Sabater [23] added this criteria to features that should be considered when working on a TMS. The authors [23] proposed a classification that goes from 0 to 2, where:

- 0: indicates that all agents in the system are considered reliable;
- 1: indicates that agents may hide or add a bias to the information but without lying;
- 2: the TMS considers that agents may be malicious and lie intentionally.

Other studies such as [11,22] classify attacks against TMS as:

- "Bad mouthing" consists in spreading false information against some agents in order to deny their reputation.
- By contrast the "good-mouthing" can be used to spread "faulty good" information on a malicious agent (example: self-promoting).
- The "On-Off attack" consists for a node to alternate between normal and malicious behaviour in order to enhance its own trust indicators between attacks.
- The "selective attack" consists for an agent to behave normally with the majority of agents in order to keep a positive reputation and then to be malicious only against some selected agents.
- The "white washing" attack is made possible in systems where an agent can make the most of the system. Then, when his reputation is too much low, he quits the system and connects again under a new identity.

2.5   Constraints

Three main constraints can be identified for embedded EMAS: available energy, computing power and memory space. These constraints should be taken into account when designing a TMS for such systems.

2.6   Trust in Embedded and Distributed Pervasive Systems

This overview of existing solutions to TMS in embedded and distributed systems is limited to completely distributed solutions. Indeed, such solutions are more scalable and fit better the objectives of EMAS. They can be applied to systems like WSNs, IoT... These solutions can be classified into three main groups: routing-based, data-centric and service-oriented solutions.

Routing-based solutions can use neighborhood monitoring approaches like in [17] (TARP protocol) [12] (EMPIRE protocol) where each agent monitors the ratio of received and sent messages from its neighbours. The EMPIRE solution tries to lower energy consumption by introducing periodic monitoring, and considers white washing and good mouthing attacks.

In data-centric solutions, [14] presents a data aggregation-based solution, RDAT, that aims at determining the number of malicious actions in the system. Agent reputation is used to limit bad/good mouthing attacks. In RDAT, energy used for computing trust levels is taken into account but not the energy necessary for monitoring actions.

Service-oriented solutions are presented in [3,4,13] for service-based IoT systems. They use social interactions within such systems for determining agent reputations. They can protect against On/Off attacks.

This overview of main types of existing TMS for pervasive systems shows that energy consumption is seldom considered, although this can be an important constraint for such systems. This is why, our approach, introduced below, considers energy levels and energy management within TMS, providing what we call an energy-aware TMS.

3   A Multi-Armed Bandit Learning Based Approach

The amount of information needed to allow an agent to make right trust decisions depends on the context. TMS are widely used in wireless sensor networks in order to allow sensor agents to choose which of their neighbours to cooperate with in order to route messages (as in [26]). These sensor agents may have multiple ways to get information about their neighbours. Indeed, a sensor agent can:

- listen that messages sent to a neighbour are forwarded to the next hop. This approach doesn't require a lot of energy but it only provides little information about neighbours.
- monitor all messages received by its neighbours and verify that they are forwarded correctly. This approach can give a lot more information to the agent about his neighbours. However, it will require the agent him to continuously listen and process all messages sent in its neighbourhood. As a consequence, this approach may make the agent greatly consume its resources and reduce its live time.
- exchange trust values with its neighbours. The information gathered this way will have a cost in terms of energy depending on the number of queried neighbours, and since this information can be manipulated by malicious agents it may not always be worth it to gather and use it. When an agent is in a trustworthy environment (i.e. with few and naive malicious agents that always behave badly) the agent will be able to identify the malicious agents only based on its interactions with them. But in case malicious agents are more intelligent (for example, they use selective or On-Off attacks) reliable agents may need to communicate with each other in order to collect enough information to avoid being betrayed. In addition, in situations where most of the recommenders are also malicious, the agent may have to spend a lot of energy to monitor other agents.

Our work aims at giving an agent the ability to adapt itself and its behaviour (in gathering information) to an unknown context while being aware of the available amount of energy. In practice, the agent must learn which behaviour gives the most reliable interactions with other agents before it runs out of energy. This problem can easily me modelled as a learning problem. Indeed, the agent has to choose between options (behaviours) that have unknown utilities (unknown performances and costs). As a consequence, the agent can only learn which option is the best. In order to easily model the different existing options to an agent, one suited learning model is the multi-armed bandit model (as promoted in [2]). We describe below how to use this model to solve our issue.

3.1 Budgeted Multi-Armed Bandit

The Multi-Armed Bandit (MAB) problem as described in [20] is a sequential decision making problem where an agent has to choose sequentially between a set of options (a set of slot machines). After making a choice (pulling the arm of a slot machine), the agent gets a reward that depends on the chosen option. The reward gain is random and unknown to the agent before his choice. The budgeted version of the multi-armed bandit problem introduces a cost function when choosing an option and a budget, thus limiting the number of plays for a given agent, whereas in the original version the agent would have played an infinite number of times. The goal of the budgeted multi-armed bandit algorithm is to maximise the reward gain of the agent before its budget runs out.

More formally, the budgeted multi-armed bandit problem can be stated as follow:

Definition 1 (Budgeted Multi-Armed Bandit Setup). *Let* $K = [\![1, k]\!]$ *with* $k \in \mathbb{N}$ *be a set of options (i.e. a set of arms),*

T a set of rounds,

$B \in \mathbb{R}$ a budget,

$\forall i \in K, \forall t \in T$, let $r_i(t)$ be the reward value obtained for choosing choice i at round t.

$\forall i \in K, \forall t \in T$, rewards $r_i(t)$ are drawn independently. But given an option $j \in K, \forall t \in T$, rewards $r_j(t)$ are drawn from random variables following the same distribution.

$\forall i \in K, \forall t \in T$, let $c_i(t)$ be the cost value payed for choosing option i at round t.

The budgeted MAB problem has been studied with different setups depending on the cost distributions of each option. For example, [25] studied a setup where the cost of an option is fixed and an agent only needs to choose each option once in order to know its cost. [6] worked on a setup where the costs of the options are randomly drawn but can only take discrete values. Later, [28] described a solution for random continuous costs.

Definition 2 (Budgeted Multi-Armed Bandit Algorithm). *A budgeted MAB algorithm A is a finite sequence of options $(i_t)_{t \in T'}$ (where T' is a finite subset of T) that aim at maximising the expected reward:*

$$E^A = \mathbb{E}\left[\sum_{t \in T'} r_{i_t}(t)\right]$$

such that

$$\sum_{t \in T'} c_{i_t}(t) \leq B$$

In practice, budgeted MAB algorithm are not evaluated in terms of their expected reward but in terms of the *regret* (see Definition 3 below) which is defined as the difference with the expected reward of an optimal algorithm (an optimal algorithm is an algorithm that can obtain the maximum reward knowing the reward and cost distributions of each option).

Definition 3. *The regret of a budgeted MAB algorithm is defined as:*

$$R^A = E^* - E^A$$
$$= E^* - \mathbb{E}\left[\sum_{t \in T'} r_{i_t}(t)\right]$$

where E^* is the expected reward of the optimal algorithm.

3.2   Taking into Account TMS Energy Consumption in MAB

To model the energy saving in TMS as a budgeted MAB problem we need to identify four elements: (i) the arms, (ii) the reward and (ii) the cost of pulling an arm, and (iv) the budget.

The possible behaviours of an agent with regards to the TMS will be the arms of our multi-armed bandit. A behaviour is defined as an ordered set of actions that include all aspects of TMS, which are: gathering trust information about other agents, evaluating them, selecting and interacting with other agents. To come back to our WSN example, we identified three behaviours:

- a naive or one-by-one behaviour: the agent uses just its own experience;
- a cooperative behaviour: the agent exchanges trust information with other agents;
- and a suspicious or checking behaviour: the agent monitors other agents.

Note that it is possible to identify more behaviours and more complex ones, but for sake of simplicity, we consider only the behaviours described above.

As our approach aims at learning how to get the maximum number of good interactions before the energy of the agent runs out, the reward given by a behaviour will be the number of good interactions obtained while using this behaviour, the cost of a behaviour will be the energy spent while using this behaviour and last, the budget will be the total amount of energy of the agent (see Table 1).

Table 1. Identified elements of the used MAB

Arm	Behaviour
Reward	Number of good interactions
Cost	Energy spend
Budget	Energy supply

3.3   Case Study

Our case study is a multi-agent system toy problem. It consists of a set of harvester agents that can collect resources located on a map and bring them back to a base station. these agents can only carry one resource at a time. In order to know where the resources are, they have access to several explorer agents that provide the service of finding the resources. When a harvester agent selects an explorer agent, the explorer will find one resource and gives its location to the harvester so this one can collect it. Our agents only have a limited supply of energy and must collect the maximum number of resources before running out of energy.

We consider an attacker that wants to disrupt the system in a denial of service fashion. The attacker can use malicious or corrupted explorer agents to indicate a position where there is no resource to make harvester agents unnecessarily go back and forth and waste their energy.

Trust Management System. In order to defend themselves from untrustworthy service providers, our agents use a TMS. We choose the TMS designed for IoT devices in a service-oriented architecture described in [13]. The TMS makes use of two information sources, which are direct information, and indirect information. Direct information takes the form of a binary value based on the result of a requested service (good or bad). Indirect information is obtained by regularly sending all the trust values to other agents.

Trust values are ratings ranging from 1 to −1 and are updated as described below:

- After agent A requested a service to a service provider agent SP, A evaluates the service as good or bad and updates the trust value of SP using Eq. 1. W_s is a weight factor depending on the requested service and the desired speed of convergence of trust. In our example we choose $W_s = 0.01$ which is the value used by the authors in [13].

$$NewTrust_{SP}^A = \begin{cases} min(1, Trust_{SP}^A + W_s) & \text{if service is good} \\ max(-1, Trust_{SP}^A - 2 * W_s) & \text{if service is bad} \end{cases} \quad (1)$$

– After agent A receives trust value from an agent R about service provider agent SP, the trust value of SP is updated using Eq. 2 and trust value of R is updated using Eq. 3. α, β and θ are thresholds used to filter bad recommendations. We choose $\alpha = 0.2$, $\beta = 0.4$ and $\theta = 0.5$, which are again the values used by the authors in [13].

$$NewTrust_{SP}^A = \begin{cases} Trust_{SP}^A + Trust_{SP}^R * Q_r & \text{if } Trust_R^A > \beta \cap Q_r \geq \alpha \\ Trust_{SP}^A & \text{otherwise} \end{cases} \quad (2)$$

$$NewTrust_R^A = \begin{cases} min(1, Trust_R^A + Q_r * \theta) & \text{if } Q_r \geq \alpha \\ max(1, Trust_R^A - Q_r * \theta) & \text{otherwise} \end{cases} \quad (3)$$

where $Q_r = 1 - |Trust_{SP}^A - Trust_{SP}^R|$.

Agent Behaviour. Our agent can implement three different behaviours that we call one-by-one behaviour, cooperative behaviour and checking behaviour.

The one-by-one behaviour described in Fig. 2 consists, for an agent, in choosing one service provider at a time based on direct experience, and collecting the resources found by the service provider. This behaviour is the most efficient in a context where most of the agents are trustworthy because all the energy spent is used to collect resources. But if the agent selects a malicious agent, it loses all the energy needed to go to the resource location and come back.

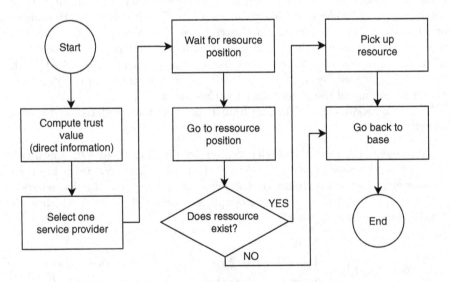

Fig. 2. Naive behaviour

The checking behaviour consists for an agent, in selecting multiple service providers at once and waiting for them to find resources. Then, instead of collecting resources one by one, when collecting the first resource the agent makes a detour to check if the other resources found by the service providers actually exit. Once the agent have checked all the resources, it can collect one by one only the existing ones. This behaviour is described in Fig. 3. Note that this behaviour is better than the first only in the case where the agent is facing a lot of malicious agents that perform complex attacks such as the On-Off attack or a selective attack.

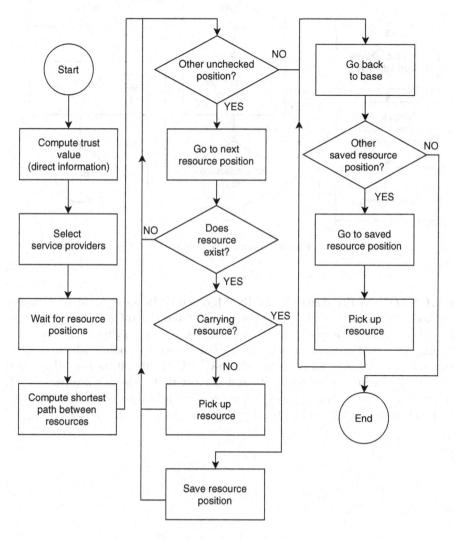

Fig. 3. Checking behaviour

The last behaviour described in Fig. 4 is called the cooperative behaviour. In this behaviour, the agent will again select the service providers one-by-one but not only using its own experience, but also by asking recommendations to other agents. If the decisions made by the agent with this behaviour aren't better than the naive behaviour, this behaviour will be less efficient due to the energy cost needed for communications.

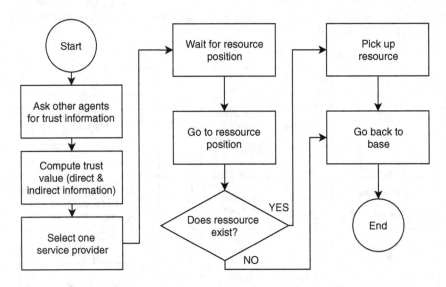

Fig. 4. Cooperative behaviour

b-GREEDY Multi-Armed Bandit Algorithm. In order to allow an agent to choose between the behaviours, we implemented the b-GREEDY algorithm described in [28]. We made this choice because this algorithm is designed for dealing with continuous random cost. To our knowledge, only [1,28] deal with this kind of cost. We have chosen the b-GREEDY algorithm over the other possibilities because of its simplicity and the fact that it doesn't involve a lot of calculations (square root and logarithm) as the others do. Also [28] shows that its performance in terms of regret are equivalent to other algorithms.

The b-GREEDY algorithm works as shown in Algorithm 1.

Algorithm 1: b-GREEDY [28]

  Input: Hyper parameter $\alpha(> 0)$

1   $t \leftarrow 1$;

2   **while** *Budget has not been run out* **do**

3      $\epsilon_t \leftarrow min\{1, \alpha K/t\}$;

4      $r \leftarrow rand([0,1])$;

       /* r is drawn from a continuous uniform distribution with

         support in $[0,1]$ */

5   **if** $r < 1 - \epsilon_t$ **then**

6        $i \leftarrow \arg \max_{k \in [1,K]} (\bar{r}_k(t)/\bar{c}_k(t))$;

         /* $\bar{r}_k(t)$ (respectively $\bar{c}_k(t)$) is the average reward

           received (respectively cost payed) from arm k at

           round t, so i is the arm with the best average

           reward-to-cost ratio   */

7   **else**

8        $i \leftarrow rand\ int(K)$;

         /* i is a randomly chosen arm   */

9   **end**

10   Play arm i;

11   Update $\bar{r}_i(t), \bar{c}_i(t)$ and the budget;

12     $t \leftarrow t + 1$;

13 **end**

3.4   Results

In order to give a proof of concept of our solution, we simulated our case study using the Multi-Agent Software Hardware simulator (MASH) platform [9].

The setup used in the simulation was the following:

- Resources were randomly placed on a square map of 50 m by 50 m;
- Moving 1 m costs a harvester agent 0.03% of its total energy;
- Sending and receiving one message from an other agent costs the harvester agent 0.01% of its total energy.

We evaluated the three different behaviours considered in this work and our solution in two different situations:

- The first situation consisted of 30 harvester agents and 50 honest explorer agents;
- The second situation consisted of 30 harvester agents, 25 honest explorer agents and 25 malicious explorer agents. In this situation malicious explorer were lying every time they were selected to find resources.

Table 2 shows the average number of resources collected by the agents in each situation using respectively the naive behaviour, the cooperative behaviour, the checking behaviour, and the proposed learning MAB algorithm. Figures 5 and 6 show respectively, in situation 1 and situation 2, how the agents choose their behaviours using our solution.

Table 2. Average number of resources collected per harvester agent

	Naive	Cooperative	Checking	MAB
Situation 1	57	28	34	40
Situation 2	27	40	34	32

In situation 1, we can see from Table 2 that the naive behaviour performs better than the two others. This is due to the fact that in this situation, there are no malicious agents; so all the energy of the agents can be used to collect resources and using an amount of energy for the TMS will reduce their performances. We can see from Fig. 5 that in situation 1, agents using our solution learn that the naive behaviour is the best and choose it more often as the time passes.

In situation 2, the cooperative behaviour becomes better than the two others because agents need to rapidly identify the malicious agents. But we can see from Fig. 6 that the advantages given by the cooperative behaviour aren't enough to let the agents learn which behaviour is the best.

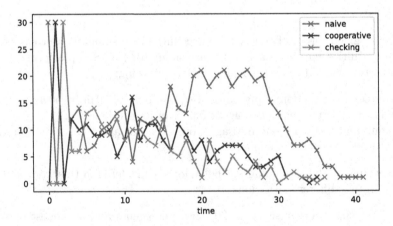

Fig. 5. Number of agents using each behaviour as a function of time in situation 1

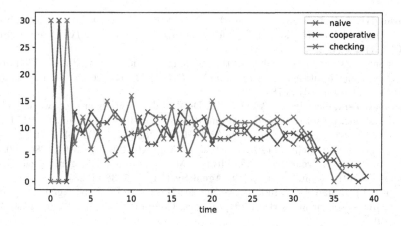

Fig. 6. Number of agents using each behaviour as a function of time in situation 2

4   Conclusion and Future Work

After motivating the need for a TMS in embedded MAS, we showed that such a TMS would have to deal with energy limitations of embedded agents. We then proposed a solution to help agents manage their energy consumption due while using trust management by making them learn when and how to gather information about potential interaction partners.

In order to make our solution really applicable, we still need to test it in more complex situations where malicious agents can launch more complex attacks such as On-Off attacks. But we also need to consider situations were recommenders (other harvester agents) can be malicious too.

References

1. Badanidiyuru, A., Kleinberg, R., Slivkins, A.: Bandits with knapsacks. In: 2013 IEEE 54th Annual Symposium on Foundations of Computer Science, pp. 207–216. IEEE (2013)
2. Bonnefoi, R., Besson, L., Moy, C., Kaufmann, E., Palicot, J.: Multi-armed bandit learning in IoT networks: learning helps even in non-stationary settings. In: Marques, P., Radwan, A., Mumtaz, S., Noguet, D., Rodriguez, J., Gundlach, M. (eds.) CrownCom 2017. LNICST, vol. 228, pp. 173–185. Springer, Cham (2018). https://doi.org/10.1007/978-3-319-76207-4_15
3. Chen, R., Bao, F., Guo, J.: Trust-based service management for social internet of things systems. IEEE Trans. Dependable Secure Comput. **13**(6), 684–696 (2016)
4. Chen, R., Guo, J., Bao, F.: Trust management for SOA-based IoT and its application to service composition. IEEE Trans. Serv. Comput. **9**(3), 482–495 (2016)
5. Cho, J.H., Chan, K., Adali, S.: A survey on trust modeling. ACM Comput. Surv. (CSUR) **48**(2), 28 (2015)
6. Ding, W., Qin, T., Zhang, X.D., Liu, T.Y.: Multi-armed bandit with budget constraint and variable costs. In: Twenty-Seventh AAAI Conference on Artificial Intelligence (2013)

7. Granatyr, J., Botelho, V., Lessing, O.R., Scalabrin, E.E., Barthès, J.P., Enembreck, F.: Trust and reputation models for multiagent systems. ACM Comput. Surv. (CSUR) **48**(2), 27 (2015)

8. Jamont, J., Occello, M.: Meeting the challenges of decentralised embedded applications using multi-agent systems. IJAOSE **5**(1), 22–68 (2015). https://doi.org/10.1504/IJAOSE.2015.078435

9. Jamont, J.-P., Occello, M., Mendes, E.: Decentralized intelligent real world embedded systems: a tool to tune design and deployment. In: Demazeau, Y., Ishida, T., Corchado, J.M., Bajo, J. (eds.) PAAMS 2013. LNCS (LNAI), vol. 7879, pp. 133–144. Springer, Heidelberg (2013). https://doi.org/10.1007/978-3-642-38073-0_12

10. Jennings, N.R., Sycara, K., Wooldridge, M.: A roadmap of agent research and development. Auton. Agent. Multi-Agent Syst. **1**(1), 7–38 (1998)

11. Lopez, J., Roman, R., Agudo, I., Fernandez-Gago, C.: Trust management systems for wireless sensor networks: best practices. Comput. Commun. **33**(9), 1086–1093 (2010)

12. Maarouf, I., Baroudi, U., Naseer, A.R.: Efficient monitoring approach for reputation system-based trust-aware routing in wireless sensor networks. IET Commun. **3**(5), 846–858 (2009)

13. Mendoza, C.V.L., Kleinschmidt, J.H.: A distributed trust management mechanism for the internet of things using a multi-service approach. Wireless Pers. Commun. **103**(3), 2501–2513 (2018)

14. Ozdemir, S.: Functional reputation based reliable data aggregation and transmission for wireless sensor networks. Comput. Commun. **31**(17), 3941–3953 (2008)

15. Pinyol, I., Sabater-Mir, J.: Computational trust and reputation models for open multi-agent systems: a review. Artif. Intell. Rev. **40**(1), 1–25 (2013)

16. Ramchurn, S.D., Huynh, D., Jennings, N.R.: Trust in multi-agent systems. Knowl. Eng. Rev. **19**(1), 1–25 (2004)

17. Rezgui, A., Eltoweissy, M.: μRACER: a reliable adaptive service-driven efficient routing protocol suite for sensor-actuator networks. IEEE Trans. Parallel Distrib. Syst. **20**(5), 607–622 (2009)

18. Ries, S.: Engineering trust in ubiquitous computing. In: Proceedings of Workshop on Software Engineering Challenges for Ubiquitous Computing, Lancaster, UK (2006)

19. Ries, S., Kangasharju, J., Mühlhäuser, M.: A classification of trust systems. In: Meersman, R., Tari, Z., Herrero, P. (eds.) OTM 2006. LNCS, vol. 4277, pp. 894–903. Springer, Heidelberg (2006). https://doi.org/10.1007/11915034_114

20. Robbins, H.: Some aspects of the sequential design of experiments. Bull. Am. Math. Soc. **58**(5), 527–535 (1952)

21. da Rocha Costa, A.C., Hübner, J.F., Bordini, R.H.: On entering an open society. In: XI Brazilian Symposium on Artificial Intelligence, vol. 535, p. 546. Citeseer (1994)

22. Ruan, Y., Durresi, A.: A survey of trust management systems for online social communities-trust modeling, trust inference and attacks. Knowl.-Based Syst. **106**, 150–163 (2016)

23. Sabater, J., Sierra, C.: Review on computational trust and reputation models. Artif. Intell. Rev. **24**(1), 33–60 (2005)

24. Sicari, S., Rizzardi, A., Grieco, L.A., Coen-Porisini, A.: Security, privacy and trust in internet of things: the road ahead. Comput. Netw. **76**, 146–164 (2015)

25. Tran-Thanh, L., Chapman, A., de Cote, E.M., Rogers, A., Jennings, N.R.: Epsilon-first policies for budget-limited multi-armed bandits. In: Twenty-Fourth AAAI Conference on Artificial Intelligence (2010)

26. Vercouter, L., Jamont, J.P.: Lightweight trusted routing for wireless sensor networks. In: Demazeau, Y., Pěchouček, M., Corchado, J.M., Pérez, J.B. (eds.) Advances on Practical Applications of Agents and Multiagent Systems. AINSC, vol. 88, pp. 87–96. Springer, Heidelberg (2011). https://doi.org/10.1007/978-3-642-19875-5_11

27. Vercouter, L., Jamont, J.: Lightweight trusted routing for wireless sensor networks. Prog. AI 1(2), 193–202 (2012). https://doi.org/10.1007/s13748-012-0017-7

28. Xia, Y., et al.: Finite budget analysis of multi-armed bandit problems. Neurocomputing 258, 13–29 (2017)

29. Yu, H., Shen, Z., Leung, C., Miao, C., Lesser, V.R.: A survey of multi-agent trust management systems. IEEE Access 1, 35–50 (2013)

30. Yu, Y., Li, K., Zhou, W., Li, P.: Trust mechanisms in wireless sensor networks: attack analysis and countermeasures. J. Netw. Comput. Appl. 35(3), 867–880 (2012)

Addressing Security Properties in Systems of Systems: Challenges and Ideas

Miguel Angel Olivero[1,2](✉) , Antonia Bertolino[1] ,
Francisco José Dominguez-Mayo[2,3] , María José Escalona[2,3] ,
and Ilaria Matteucci[4]

[1] Istituto di Scienza e Tecnologie dell'Informazione,
Consiglio Nazionale delle Ricerche, Pisa, Italy
{miguelangel.olivero, antonia.bertolino}@isti.cnr.it
[2] Web Engineering and Early Testing (IWT2) Research Group,
Universidad de Sevilla, Seville, Spain
{fjdominguez, mjescalona}@us.es
[3] Computer Languages and System Department,
Universidad de Sevilla, Seville, Spain
[4] Istituto di Informatica e Telematica,
Consiglio Nazionale delle Ricerche, Pisa, Italy
ilaria.matteucci@iit.cnr.it

Abstract. Within growing pervasive information systems, Systems of Systems (SoS) emerge as a new research frontier. A SoS is formed by a set of constituent systems that live on their own with well-established functionalities and requirements, and, in certain circumstances, they must collaborate to achieve a common mission. In this scenario, security is one crucial property that needs to be considered since the early stages of SoS lifecycle. Unfortunately, SoS security cannot be guaranteed by addressing the security of each constituent system separately. The aim of this paper is to discuss the challenges faced in addressing the security of SoS and to propose some research ideas centered around the notion of a mission to be carried out by the SoS.

Keywords: Mission-oriented modeling and testing · Security ·
System of Systems

1 Introduction

The challenge of governing the cooperation among a set of independent systems dynamically interconnected and working as a large complex system has been addressed by researchers since the early 90's [1, 2]. In recent years, this concept is referred to as a "System of Systems" (SoS) [3]. In their extensive review of SoS concepts and techniques, Nielsen and coauthors [3] provide several examples of domains where SoS becomes prevalent, including transportation networks, smart energy grids, and e-commerce applications, with emergency management remaining the most evident case in which SoS are extensively used [4].

© Springer Nature Switzerland AG 2019
R. Calinescu and F. Di Giandomenico (Eds.): SERENE 2019, LNCS 11732, pp. 138–146, 2019.
https://doi.org/10.1007/978-3-030-30856-8_10

A SoS aims at achieving global goals that would be infeasible for its constituent systems working in isolation. Such SoS goals have been named as *missions* [5]. The conceptual model of a mission drives the representation of the SoS emergent behavior, such as, among others, the involved tasks and constraints, the mission trigger, the executor systems, and so on [6]. Indeed, SoS missions are a key component when modeling or validating an SoS, as well as when defining its architecture.

Silva and coauthors have proposed mKAOS [5], which is both a mission-oriented language and an approach for modeling and designing SoS. The approach is based on the Goal Oriented Requirements Engineering, or GORE [7]. The mKAOS language extends KAOS/SysML (a language provided by the Object Management Group) and allows to assign a set of missions to each constituent system in the SoS. In this language, the sum of all joint works of the systems describes the functionality of the whole system.

However, the problem of modeling and addressing non-functional properties of SoS is not covered by mKAOS so far, and still remains largely unexplored [8]. In particular, concerning security, Ki-Aries and coauthors state that there exists *"no clear guidance or limited tool-support integrating different modelling elements to visualize and assess the SoS security consequences"* [9].

To address this need, we aim at modeling SoS security requirements in the context of SoS missions. Once the security requirements have been established, we also aim at validating the possible different SoS solutions, by means of an appropriate testing campaign. In fact, also concerning SoS security testing we identified a gap in current literature: to the best of our knowledge a specific approach addressing SoS security testing does not yet exist.

Summarizing, our research tackles security challenges on SoS and considers using a mission-oriented security modeling and testing approach that we refer to as Testing for Security in System of Systems (TeSSoS). We briefly introduced all steps that compose TeSSoS in [10] and stated the purposes of this method. In this paper, we lay the wider scene for such research, providing motivations, and discussing relevant challenges. In particular, we discuss the differences when addressing the security among different SoS architectures and how these challenges could be addressed. For completeness, we also include an outline of the on-going approach TeSSoS [10].

This paper is organized as follows: Sect. 2 revises existing SoS architectures by distinguishing how the different constituent systems organize themselves to achieve a common goal. It also discusses their particular security issues and describes the identified challenges for each SoS architecture. Section 3 discusses about the depicted scenarios and introduces the TeSSoS approach to assess the security in SoS that includes modelling and testing. Finally, the conclusions of our work are in Sect. 4.

2 Security Issues in Systems of Systems

Security is among the most relevant and critical features of SoS. It is a special concern for researchers in the military domain and in the Information Technology area as well [11]. The main challenge in analyzing and testing security properties in SoS derives from the non-compositional nature of security properties. In fact, guaranteeing the security of each constituent component of the SoS does not guarantee that the SoS is secure as a whole.

Indeed, one of the main aspects of SoS is that they are dynamically evolving. The constituents that compose the SoS may change at any time, or some new systems may be added to the environment or removed. Hence, when assessing the quality of a SoS and its evolution, it is important to consider any mechanism able to guarantee security and avoid as many vulnerabilities and weaknesses as possible, for example when new systems join. the target SoS.

Every SoS has four general interdependency threats [12]:

(1) A constituent system failure;
(2) A constituent system impersonation;
(3) Communication channel failure;
(4) Communication channel infection.

Additionally, a fifth threat is introduced when constituents are sharing data. This vulnerability arises because by merging partial results coming from different constituent systems, more information becomes available and can be exploited for an SoS attack. Perhaps the constituent systems are sharing data, that, taken in isolation, are meaningless. However, when combining the set of data available from more systems, valuable information can be generated in a synergic way that can compromise the SoS.

In the literature four different architectures of SoS have been defined: Directed, Acknowledged, Collaborative, and Virtual [13, 14]. Figure 1 summarizes the process for categorizing the system according to its key features. By knowing about the existence of a central entity and the existence of guidelines, SoS can be organized in any of the four categories. The key factor that distinguishes one architecture from another is how they communicate and interact among them: the security issues that may affect an SoS vary depending on its architecture. In a similar way, testing each SoS is different depending on the architecture because of the nature, that require a different responsible for managing the security. In the remainder of this section, we discuss such security issues in the four different SoS architectures.

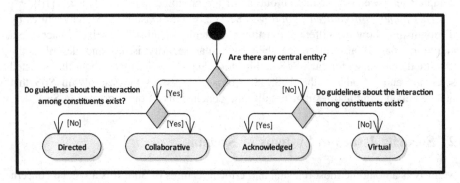

Fig. 1. SoS architecture decision tree

For the sake of understanding, using an airport as a fil rouge, for each architecture we supply different scenarios related to distinct subsystems of an airport as examples of SoS.

2.1 Directed SoS

Directed SoSs are managed by a central system that handles the success of the global purpose. Each constituent system is independent, but prioritizes the tasks commanded by the central. An example of a Directed SoS is the airport's system of surveillance, where each part, such as cameras infrastructures, or boarding pass scanners, are independent on their own when disconnected from the SoS, however these systems receive and execute commands according to precise guidelines when are integrated in the SoS.

Security testing in Directed SoS is the simplest case. It relies on the communication of each constituent system with the central one, which is responsible of security negotiation among constituent systems.

Indeed, by having a central entity that manages all the communications, security requirements and properties can be managed in a centralized way. The constituents can be centrally organized not only to achieve the final goal, but also to satisfy security requirements. The latter will require monitoring (in both, active and passive way) the communications among constituents, and the behavior of each constituent as well. Note that governing the set of security requirements of a Directed SoS may require a negotiation phase among the constituents.

The main challenge for the security when using this kind of architecture is to establish the common criteria that define the shared concept of security. In this sense, every system that would coordinate with the central entity must agree with the security requirements. Given the fact that every constituent system needs to communicate with the central entity, a strategy based on access control may be helpful to avoid unauthorized use of resources.

2.2 Collaborative SoS

An SoS is Collaborative when, even being coordinated by a central authority, the constituent systems retain self-control. The constituents are advised by the central system, but the final decision upon their actions is taken by the constituent systems themselves. Referring again to the Airport example, the landing track can be seen as an Collaborative SoS. The central system is the command tower, each system knows every other one; there are some passive systems, but there are others that maintain their independence, the planes.

As in the case of the Directed SoS, the central entity can select and coordinate the constituents in such a way that security requirements are satisfied by the emergent SoS. Conversely with respect to the Directed SoS case, the central entity is not able to monitor or correct potential insecure behaviors of the constituents.

Furthermore, the SoS lacks control on the behavior of each single constituent. The data shared with the constituent systems may be manipulated by functionalities out of the scope of the SoS, which introduces vulnerabilities on the privacy of the SoS data.

Challenges for this architecture include the ones defined for Directed SoS. However, since these systems retain independence, and are not strictly controlled by the central system, it would be possible for a constituent system to use information from other constituent systems for its own purposes, intentionally or unintentionally. This problem introduces the need of clearly stating which are the essential data each constituent requires, to avoid providing data that are not strictly necessary. In security-related scientific literature the fact of not sharing more than strictly needed data, is known as non-disclosure or data sharing agreement. Nevertheless, in the event of an attack, the attacker could access data shared among the different constituents and reconstruct sensitive information about the SoS, that may be used to exploit its security in other attacks.

Testing the security in Collaborative SoS is like the Directed SoS security testing since there is a central system that helps in the negotiation of the security among the constituent systems. However, despite the architecture is similar, the number of vulnerabilities to test on the SoS increases. This is produced in part by the need of trusting other constituents as well as testing the final purpose of the SoS. It is necessary to define mechanisms for testing the communication that each constituent system performs with other constituents, as well as the functionality or behavior of the systems when processing data from the SoS. These tests should aim at discovering if there are any potential data leaks that combined with other data can reveal information that jeopardizes the security of SoS.

2.3 Acknowledged SoS

Acknowledged SoS are not controlled by a central system, but they may abide by an agreement on performing certain tasks. Acknowledged SoS in the airport context could be transport services such as the taxi company, or the autobuses. There is no common entity that manages all of them, notwithstanding they know each other and know they are somehow cooperating to allow people timely reach their destinations.

Managing the security in this kind of architecture requires a distributed and decentralized organization. Each constituent oversees the mutual agreements and should cooperate and coordinate with the others. In this architecture, a security requirements negotiation phase is essential. Additionally, each constituent must guarantee to behave correctly, i.e., in a compliant way with respect to the set of agreed requirements.

Challenges from Directed and Acknowledged architectures are also present in this one. However, given the fact that there is not a central entity to coordinate, but a common goal to achieve, individual interests of the systems may arise and create security vulnerabilities. Privacy could be also affected in this architecture. Constituent systems may change from a SoS to another according to their availability. When doing joint work, systems share data and functionalities, however, some systems may make an improper use of the collective data for their own or third parties' profit. Thus, lack of trust and/or lack of responsibilities among the constituent systems in an acknowledged architecture could become a considerable risk as for the shared data and functionalities.

Hence testing acknowledged SoS is more complex than in the previous cases. The lack of a central system helping in the negotiation of the security requirements makes an extensive coordination process necessary, in which each system shall conduct this negotiation on its own sake.

During a collaboration, the systems may generate a cascade problem [15], which may occur when a system with high security levels is sharing data with a system with lower security. In other words, a different level of security among constituent systems, causes that the system with lower security level become the weakest link in the SoS. At the time of working in this architecture, an extensive analysis of the constituent systems must be executed to detect the weakest systems and determine if any of them could create the cascade problem. The chain of systems may be extended to deeper levels, analyzing also other SoS on which each constituent system is also working.

2.4   Virtual SoS

Virtual SoS emerge in unpredictable ways, as an outcome of the results coming from individual systems. They are not coordinated by a central system and the systems may not even know that they are working for a global purpose. An example of this architecture in the airport context is a set of shops in the duty-free section. These shops do not know about each other if it is not necessary, and they do not have a common purpose to achieve.

Managing the security in this architecture needs a distributed and decentralized organization. There are no formal agreements among the shops, but they are providing services for clients who may combine the items that these different shops offer. This is the architecture that may present more difficulties when analyzing its vulnerabilities with respect to security, because there is neither a central entity that may guarantee security nor an agreement that describes which should be the correct behavior. On the other hand, exactly because they collaborate loosely, the vulnerabilities might have minimal impact on each single system on average. The trust is not considered on this architecture, and the purpose of the global mission does not conditionate the functionalities of each single constituent.

Security requirements cannot be easily tested in virtual SoS because there is uncertainty about how the constituent systems would communicate in the future, however it could be analyzed considering previous SoS collaborations. In SoS architectures, pieces of data from different systems may be put together and produce information that exposes the security of another. Despite this, Virtual architecture might provide the same challenges as the previous architectures and include an additional one, the inability of knowing what are those systems that could provide such pieces of data. To the best of our knowledge, no defensive mechanisms can be clearly defined for addressing this problem, but contingency plans can be defined to mitigate an exploitation of the security.

3   Addressing Security

Our work aims at providing a method to address the security issues arising in the SoS architecture. The method, named Testing for Security in System of Systems (TeSSoS) [10], focuses in modeling the security requirements of the SoS and generating the test cases to evaluate the security. TeSSoS is an ongoing work that has been designed as a set of five stages. At each stage, guidelines are supplied to assess the security challenges emerging in the SoS under exam.

3.1 Modeling Security of System of Systems

Models in SoS are dynamic because an SoS is constantly evolving. Every new incoming system arriving into the SoS needs to be analyzed to keep some standard security level among the constituent systems.

To model the security in SoS, as in isolated systems, it is necessary to consider threats, vulnerabilities, weaknesses, attackers, and attacks that affect the assets. In this view, we are modeling the security and the synergic features of the constituent systems in the SoS. To address the modeling of the security we consider an SoS already modelled with its functional features. On this basis, to model the security properties, it is mandatory to analyze the communication among each constituent system, channels, and their contents, and study the activities that each system performs over these communication channels.

The first three stages in the TeSSoS approach target the SoS modeling and the security analysis. The first one is SoS Discovery that focuses on the SoS modeling, eliciting the constituent systems agreements, and defining the assets. In the second stage, called Red Requirements, the SoS model and its vulnerabilities are analyzed. Red Requirements were designed to allow reusing the modeled vulnerabilities to be addressed so these can be used as test cases. In this way, Red Requirements are also used to evaluate if vulnerabilities have been solved. As a result, a catalog of potential attacks is produced and written in Gherkin[1] language, which is ready for testing stages. Third, Blue Requirements supply counter-measures to avoid earlier identified vulnerabilities to succeed. Human training is also considered as a countermeasure to avoid attacks since the human factor is the one that affects the most security properties.

The SoS models, the detected vulnerabilities and proposed improvements are defined in the three first phases of TeSSoS. The method continues with systems development and the humans training. The Blue Requirements provide the catalog of User Stories ready to be developed for the development team of each constituent system according to their responsibilities in an agile environment [16]. However, some difficulties may arise when developing or training, since systems in the SoS can be managed by third parties.

3.2 Testing the Security of System of Systems

In the SoS context it is common to find third-party black-box systems among the constituent systems.

Given that security is a non-compositional feature, and the security of the SoS does not depend only on the security of the constituent systems, testing the security in SoS is

---

[1] https://cucumber.io/docs/reference#gherkin.

not just testing the security on each single constituent system, but testing the communication among the constituents.

The TeSSoS approach includes a testing phase after the development and training. The design of the test cases is not necessary since it is possible to reuse the Red Requirements definition as test cases. This fact allows reducing testing phase just to execution and evaluation.

However, since some constituent systems may be black-box systems, we can only rely on the behavior of these systems. The tester could for instance perform the same actions an attacker or an accidental user would do in a Penetration testing [17]. Another common security testing approach that behaves in this way is Fuzz testing [18, 19]. Fuzzing works by analyzing the output and behavior of the system under test when it is stimulated with random input. This testing technique can be applied with different perspectives by considering not only to randomly modify the content messages, but also the sequence order of such messages, or apply some kind of knowledge instead of full random generation. Alternatively, we could derive a model-based approach that is based on the Red requirements model using penetration testing on which the attacker behavior is replicated [20]. This testing strategy is carried out by the so-called Red Team, which simulates an attacker.

4 Conclusions

In this work we have reviewed the security challenges over the four possible architectures of an SoS. For each identified architecture we provide some examples of how the joint work is managed using the environment of an airport.

Given their natures, each architecture has different security challenges and, according to their architecture, different approaches are identified to be addressed. To analyze the security, and to detect the potential vulnerabilities on the SoS, we introduce an ongoing work named TeSSoS. This proposal organizes a set of ordered stages that guide the process of analyzing the security in the SoS context through modeling and testing.

Considering the challenges that face the security described in this work, future work will focus in addressing the problem of modeling and testing security requirements for the SoS. To this end, the phases in the TeSSoS approach will be defined in detail with the challenges of the different architectures in mind.

Acknowledgments. This work has been partially supported by the GAUSS National Research Project (MIUR, PRIN 2015, Contract 2015KWREMX) and by the Spanish Ministry of Economy and Competitiveness (POLOLAS, TIN 2016-76956-C3-2-R).

References

1. Richardson, J.D., Wheeler, T.J.: An object oriented methodology integrating design, analysis, modelling, and simulation of systems of systems. In: 4th Annual Conference on AI, Simulation and Planning in High Autonomy Systems, pp. 238–244 (1993)
2. Bodeau, D.J.: System-of-systems security engineering. In: Proceedings of the 10th Annual Computer Security Applications Conference, pp. 228–235 (1994)
3. Nielsen, C.B., Larsen, P.G., Fitzgerald, J., Woodcock, J., Peleska, J.: Systems of systems engineering: basic concepts, model-based techniques, and research directions. ACM Comput. Surv. (CSUR) **48**(2), 18 (2015)
4. Liu, S.: Employing system of systems engineering in China's emergency management. IEEE Syst. J. **5**(2), 298–308 (2011)
5. Silva, E., Batista, T., Oquendo, F.: A mission-oriented approach for designing system-of-systems. In: SoSE, pp. 346–351 (2015)
6. Silva, E., Cavalcante, E., Batista, T., Oquendo, F., Delicato, F.C., Pires, P.F.: On the characterization of missions of systems-of-systems. In: European Conference on Software Architecture Workshops, p. 26. ACM (2014)
7. van Lamsweerde, A.: Goal-oriented requirements engineering: a guided tour. In: Proceedings of the Fifth IEEE International Symposium on Requirements Engineering, pp. 249–262 (2001)
8. Chiprianov, V., Falkner, K., Gallon, L., Munier, M.: Towards modelling and analysing non-functional properties of systems of systems. In: SOSE, pp. 289–294 (2014)
9. Ki-Aries, D., Faily, S., Dogan, H., Williams, C.: Assessing system of systems security risk and requirements with OASoSIS. In: ESPRE, pp. 14–20. IEEE (2018)
10. Olivero, M.A., Bertolino, A., Dominguez-Mayo, F.J., Escalona, M.J., Matteucci, I.: Security assessment of systems of systems. In: SESoS (2019)
11. Bianchi, T., Santos, D.S., Felizardo, K.R.: Quality attributes of systems-of-systems: a systematic literature review. In: SESoS 2015, pp. 23–30 (2015)
12. Guariniello, C., DeLaurentis, D.: Communications, information, and cyber security in systems-of-systems: assessing the impact of attacks through interdependency analysis. Procedia Comput. Sci. **28**, 720–727 (2014). CSER 2014
13. Halfond, W.G.J., Choudhary, S.R., Orso, A.: Penetration testing with improved input vector identification. In: Proceedings of the 2nd International Conference on Software Testing Verification and Validation, ICST 2009, pp. 346–355 (2009)
14. Dahmann, J.S., Baldwin, K.J.: Understanding the current state of US defense systems of systems and the implications for systems engineering. In: SysCon 2008, pp. 99–105 (2008)
15. Horton, J.D., et al.: The cascade vulnerability problem. J. Comput. Secur. **2**(4), 110–116 (1993)
16. Cohn, M.: User Stories Applied: For Agile Software Development. Addison-Wesley Profession, Boston (2004)
17. Beizer, B.: Black-box testing: techniques for functional testing of software and systems (1995)
18. Shanmugam, B., Idris, N.B.: Improved intrusion detection system using fuzzy logic for detecting anamoly and misuse type of attacks. In: 2009 ICSCPR, pp. 212–217 (2009)
19. Tian-yang, G., Yin-sheng, S., You-yuan, F.: Research on software security testing. World Acad. Sci. Eng. Technol. **69**, 647–651 (2010)
20. Bacudio, A.G., Yuan, X., Chu, B.T.B., Jones, M.: An overview of penetration testing. Int. J. Netw. Secur. Appl. **3**, 19–38 (2011)

On the Use of Quality Models to Characterize Trustworthiness Properties

Tania Basso$^{(\boxtimes)}$, Hebert Silva$^{(\boxtimes)}$, and Regina Moraes$^{(\boxtimes)}$

University of Campinas, Limeira, SP, Brazil
{taniabasso,hebert.oliveiras,regina}@ft.unicamp.br

Abstract. Making informed choices when designing or contracting a system is yet a very challenging task. One of the biggest users' concern is to select the most trustworthy solution. However, it is difficult to understand the trustworthiness of a system, because it encompasses a large diversity of properties such as security, privacy, performance, among others. Composing a measure that considers such a large number of properties, the relationship among them and their relevance in the composition requires a well defined model, such as a quality model. In this experience report, we study whether quality models can provide scores that are useful to characterize those properties, helping users to choose the most trustworthy of the available alternatives. Then, we have chosen a property that is on the top of users concerns: data privacy. Results showed a higher percentage of success of linkage attacks when the privacy score is lower, indicating the usefulness of quality models in measuring and improving data privacy and providing interesting insights to the users.

Keywords: Trustworthiness · Privacy · Quality model

1 Introduction

Nowadays, most online services requires users to provide personal and payment information, which often brings concern to them regarding trust. **Trust** is a bilateral relationship and involves a trust subject (or *trustor*) and a trust object (or *trustee*) [9]. A trust relationship between them is built on a *trust matter* within specific *trust circumstances*, which together are a *trust context*. **Trustworthiness** on the other hand has been used sometimes as a synonym for security and sometimes for dependability, but in reality it is more than that and it is commonly complemented with user experience [10]. In practice, trustworthiness can be understood as a multi-dimensional construct combining specific attributes, properties and characteristics. According to *The Industrial Internet Security Framework*, from *The Industrial Internet Consortium (IIC)*[1], resilience is one of

---

[1] https://www.iiconsortium.org.

© Springer Nature Switzerland AG 2019
R. Calinescu and F. Di Giandomenico (Eds.): SERENE 2019, LNCS 11732, pp. 147–155, 2019.
https://doi.org/10.1007/978-3-030-30856-8_11

the key system characteristics which make the system trustworthy. Trustworthiness is defined as "a degree of confidence one has that the system performs as expected with characteristics including safety, security, privacy, reliability and resilience in the face of environmental disruptions, human errors, system faults and attacks". We also advocate that trustworthiness is a much broader property that involves other properties such as dependability, fairness, transparency, scalability, just to name a few.

Trustworthiness and resilience are properties that have been considered together to ensure that more complex systems, in different contexts, achieve their goals. For example, the work of Henschke and Ford [4] highlights the importance of trustworthiness for resilient cybersystems; Kreutz et al. [8] proposed a set of tools and techniques for increasing the resilience and trustworthiness of identity providers (IdPs) based on OpenID. Kort and Rudina [7] proposed a semiformal model with trustworthiness properties definitions and their connections for IIoT system behavior.

However, in these different contexts, specially in the view of cloud service providers, it is difficult for the user to characterize trustworthiness from different providers before choosing a service, if no tool is available to support this task.

One possibility is to use **quality models**, which are proposed in the ISO/IEC 25000 (SQuaRE) standard [6] as a way to formalize the interpretation of measures and the relationship among them. These models are built by a user/analyst, who knows in advance the context, the final scores, their units and scales. This way, it is possible to define how the measures should be aggregated in the analysis, and what procedures have to be used to homogenize their values, so they can be aggregated. It is possible to define one quality model for each considered property, and then, these different perspectives can be aggregate following a hierarchical structure, as proposed in the ATMOSPHERE project[2].

In this paper, we **investigate if quality models are useful to characterize a service or system being used in different contexts where the trustworthiness is key value.** For this, we present diverse scenarios in which quality models are used to characterize the *privacy of data*, considering re-identification risk and information loss. Each of these scenarios is demonstrated with real datasets and experiments, which allowed to exercise the quality models and analyzed whether the scores they provide represent a good characterization of a service or system regarding data privacy.

The results showed that the use of quality models to calculate privacy scores can be useful to identify the best anonymity level considering the trade-off between data privacy and data utility.

The paper is organized as follows. Section 2 presents the background on data anonymization, measures and scores and the quality model concepts. Section 3 shows how to instantiate the quality model for data privacy and the application of the instance to eight real datasets. Section 4 presents the lessons learned through the experiments and the conclusions.

---

[2] https://www.atmosphere-eubrazil.eu/.

2   Background and Quality Model Concepts

This section introduces key concepts addressed by the work regarding anonymization and the Logic Score of Preferences (LSP) method, as well as related work that support the motivation of the proposal.

2.1   Data Anonymization and PRIVAaaS Framework

Data Anonymization (or de-identification), consists of techniques that can be applied on data to prevent the recovery of individual information. An anonymous record or transaction prevents data, individually or combined with other data, to be associated with a particular subject. Three categories of attributes can be found in each record in a database, in light of the disclosure risks: (i) identifiers (attributes that uniquely identify individuals, e.g., ID, name, social security number); (ii) quasi-identifiers (attributes that can be combined with external information to expose some individuals, or to reduce uncertainty about their identities, e.g., birth date, ZIP code, position, job, blood type); (iii) sensitive attributes (attributes that contain sensitive information about individuals, e.g., salary, medical examinations, credit card releases).

There are several anonymization techniques that can be applied on data in order to protect the privacy of individual. The most used in the context of this paper are generalization (attribute values are generalized to a range in order to reduce the granularity of representation) and suppression (the key attributes or the quasi-identifiers are removed completely to form the anonymized table). Also, anonymization models (e.g., k-anonymity, l-diversity, t-closeness, b-likeness) can be applied to avoid re-identification. The model used in this work is the k-anonymity [11]. In this model, any combination of quasi-identifier appears at least in k-records in an anonymity table. The k must be a positive integer value (greater than or equal 2) and is defined by the owner of the data.

After data set is anonymized it is important to evaluate the risk of re-identification, i.e, to analyze the proportion of records that are unique within a particular population and identify the most vulnerable records in the data set.

This work relies on PRIVAaaS framework to apply the anonymization techniques and to calculate the re-identification risk. This component is a free and open source tool, developed in Java, and suitable to big data and cloud computing context. Basically, PRIVAaaS receives as input the data to be anonymized and an anonymization policy (i.e., the file which specifies the anonymization techniques/models that must be applied to each of the fields of input data). It applies the techniques according to the policy and provides, as output, the anonymized data set.

PRIVAaaS encapsulates the ARX tool[3] to reuse its k-anonymity model implementation, to calculate the re-identification risk and data loss rates. Also, PRIVAaaS has a module that performs privacy attacks. We adopted it because it is adaptable to different platforms, addressing interoperability issues. PRIVAaaS was presented in previous work [1], where more details can be found.

---

[3] https://arx.deidentifier.org/.

2.2   The LSP Scoring Technique and Quality Model

As placed before, trustworthiness can be understood as a multi-dimensional construct combining specific attributes, properties and characteristics (for example, security, privacy, fairness, transparency, dependability, among others). All of them have other sub-attributes that enlarge a lot the possibilities to be addressed. Since several conflicting properties may be involved in the analysis, a multi-criteria decision-making (MCDM) based technique can be useful. It can be used to support and guide the comparison of the systems or components fulfilling the system requirements for a particular application and the selection among similar services or systems. So, using MCDM one can be able to define how to compute the global score of a service considering the measures, relationship among them and their relative importance considering a context of use.

Considering multiple criteria implies a complex assessment process that needs to consider, not only the individual metrics, but also their (sometimes conflicting) combinations. In this work, Logic Score of Preferences (LSP) [2] was chosen due to its previous use in the dependability field, the capability to assess and compare complex systems, to deal with attributes tradeoffs and its simplicity when compared with other similar techniques. The LSP approach, in our case, comprises multiple aggregation blocks, including defining how the different elements should be used to produce a final score.

Usually, measures of a service or system present distinct scales and dimensions, e.g., seconds or milliseconds, percentage, and so on. In order to apply LSP, the measures should be brought to the same scale before the aggregation. To do this, we used the normalization functions proposed in [3]. They use lower thresholds (for example, a minimum throughput for a server) and higher thresholds (that satisfy the requirements for which better values do not benefit the requirements as they are already fully satisfied) within the definition of quality criterion functions. The thresholds represent the range of acceptable input values (from Xmin to Xmax) of any given leaf-level attribute of the quality model. This normalization procedure establishes an equivalence between the measured value and the system quality requirements within a 0–100 quality scale. However, when normalizing an attribute, it must be considered whether it is a benefit attribute (the higher the value, the better) like throughput, or a cost attribute (the lower, the better) as memory usage. The normalization procedure uses this information to guide the normalization (for the benefit attributes 0 corresponds to the lower and 100 to the higher threshold and the inverse is applied to the cost attribute).

To use the LSP technique, it is necessary to first define a Quality Model [5], which is essentially a conceptual representation of attributes, weights, thresholds and operators that should express the requirements that the system should meet (for example, the tree structure in Fig. 1). The blocks, in this work, represent (leaf or composite) attributes, which are aggregated (by the operators). Values at the bottom level (leaf attributes) are aggregated to calculate upper level values (composite attributes), towards the calculation of the final score of the system through a single 0-to-100 score.

3   Privacy Quality Model: Anonymization and Linkage Attacks

Data privacy is one of the properties that makes up a trustworthiness system. In this work data privacy is obtained by anonymization techniques. Two main attributes are considered to compose data privacy: the re-identification risk (the probability of discovering an individual by matching anonymized data with publicly available information) and the information loss (the amount of information that can be obtained about the original values of variables in the input dataset).

Figure 1 presents a Quality Model that was instantiated for data privacy. The goal is to calculate the privacy score of a system. As can be observed, data privacy is one of the properties composing the System Trustworthiness. The figure shows also the range of the normalization values (NormalMin and Normal Max) considered in the normalization function applied on leaf attributes. This means that the values received as metric will be normalized in this range (0 up to 1), maintaining the proportion between measures. Other information highlighted in Fig. 1 are the thresholds for the attributes in any level of the model. For example, the re-identification risk accepts thresholds between 1 up to 5% and in this case it was defined based on the literature (it can rely on experts too). It means that a re-identification risk metric will be accept if it complies with this range, otherwise the anonymity level must be increased to reduce the risk.

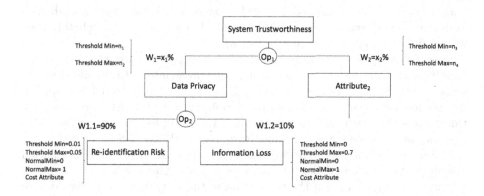

Fig. 1. Quality model instance for privacy

Because there is a trade-off between data privacy and data utility in data mining context, the other attribute that composes data privacy is the information loss. Nevertheless, re-identification risk is considered in this work much more important and it is the reason why its weight $(w_{i.j})$ was configured as 90%

while information loss receives only 10% in the composition and both are *Cost* attributes (the lower the attribute value the better for the composed score - the privacy score). The metrics can be collected several times during an experiment. So, the set of same metrics collected during the experiment composes a score. This score can be calculated considering average, sum, minimum or maximum values among this set of metrics. Particularly, for this work the average was chosen. The operation (op_2) that aggregates both leaf attributes should be chosen among neutrality (the weighted mean representing the combination of simultaneous satisfaction of requirements), simultaneity (all requirements must be satisfied implying in an *and* operation) and replaceability (the requirement that has a higher priority replaces the remaining ones implying in an *or* operation). For the privacy model in this work neutrality operation was chosen.

We used eight datasets provided by UCI[4] and Figure Eight platform[5], that are repositories used by the machine learning community. Due to space restrictions, we present the details of three of them (marked with * in Fig. 3), which present similar results to the others and may represent generalized results. They are: *Medicine Sales* (data referring to 1 month of medicines sales); *Indian Terrorism Death* (deaths mentioned in sentences from the South Asia Terrorism Portal); *New England Patriots Deflategate sentiment* (sentiment expressed in the Twitter, related to deflated footballs and whether the Patriots cheated, before 2015 Super Bowl). For the other five datasets, although we did not show all the details, the amount of tuples and the highest privacy scores are included in Fig. 3. These datasets are *Adults* (data sample extracted from the 1994 US Census database); *Internet* (contains general demographic information on US internet users collected from October through November,1997); *CMC* (subset of the 1987 National Indonesia Contraceptive Prevalence Survey), *Airlines* (Airlines Twitter data was scraped from February of 2015) and *Death* (South Asia Terrorism Portal counted the deaths mentioned in a sentence and whether they were terrorists, civilians, or security forces).

The following steps were used for all datasets in the experiment: (i) the identifiers and quasi-identifiers attributes were anonymized; (ii) in addition, the sensitive attributes were anonymized; (iii) the k-anonymity model was applied increasing k until the re-identification risk complies with the risk threshold. Risk threshold is the maximum re-identification risk accepted to the dataset. This anonymization process was performed through the PRIVAaaS framework.

After each previous described steps, the re-identication risk and information loss were calculated as well as the score of privacy. Then, linkage attacks were performed to understand if the graduation of the privacy score is aligned with more/less facility to attack success. The linkage attacks were performed by the PRIVAaaS framework on the k-anonymized datasets. In this type of attack, an adversary using some auxiliary information about a certain individual can determine which record of the database corresponds to such individual. For example, an attacker could easily use a public voter list (i.e. a public register) for cross-referencing. Figure 2 shows the privacy results.

---

[4] https://archive.ics.uci.edu/ml/datasets.html.

[5] https://www.figure-eight.com/.

Medicines Dataset								
			Risk Threshold					
Steps	ID Suppress	QuasiID Supress	100%	50%	10%	1%	0.5%	0.1%
Possibilities	1	1	2	2	5	62	62	62
# Attacks	153	153	247	247	520	5730	5730	5730
Re-identification Risk	1	1	0.33333	0.33333	0.025	0.00063131	0.00063131	0.0000307
Data Loss	0	0	0.3355	0.3355	0.509	0.8587	0.8587	0.8587
Privacy Score	0.1	0.1	0.666453	0.666453	0.9266	0.91356182	0.91356182	0.91410237
k-value	-	-	2	2	5	62	62	62

Indian Terrorism Deaths Dataset								
			Risk Threshold					
Steps	ID Suppress	QuasiID Supress	100%	50%	10%	1%	0.5%	0.1%
Possibilities	1	1	18	23	23	10362	10362	10362
# Attacks	2215	2215	26	15	15	10362	10362	10362
Re-identification Risk	1	1	0.33333	0.33333	0.0434	0.0000965	0.0000965	0.0000965
Data Loss	0	0	0.3272	0.3272	0.4142	0.8737	0.8737	0.8737
Privacy Score	0.1	0.1	0.667283	0.667284	0.91952	0.91254315	0.91254315	0.91254315
k-value	-	-	2	2	5	37	37	37

New England Patriots Deflategate Sentiment Dataset								
			Risk Threshold					
Steps	ID Suppress	QuasiID Supress	100%	50%	10%	1%	0.5%	0.1%
Possibilities	1	1	2	2	4	17	17	17
# Attacks	4735	2597	3768	3768	246	141	141	141
Re-identification Risk	1	1	0.5000	0.5000	0.0666	0.00077579	0.00077579	0.00077579
Data Loss	0	0	0.3488	0.3488	0.384	0.5874	0.5874	0.5874
Privacy Score	0.1	0.1	0.51512	0.51512	0.90166	0.94056179	0.94056179	0.94056179
k-value	-	-	2	2	4	17	17	17

Fig. 2. Results for data privacy.

Dataset	#Tuples	Privacy Score
Adults	32561	0.980620
Internet	10104	0.972480
CMC	1473	0.971000
Terrorism*	27233	0.919520
Medicine*	22586	0.926600
Airlines	16000	0.861940
Deflategate*	11814	0.940562
Deaths	2355	0.916870

Fig. 3. Databases and respective privacy scores.

In Fig. 2, the anonymization and calculation of *Re-Identification Risk, Data Loss* and *Privacy Score* were performed for different *Steps*: (i) only the identifiers were suppressed (*ID Suppress*); (ii) the Quasi identifiers were also suppressed (*QuasiID Suppress*); in the next steps the (*Risk Threshold*) was tuned from 100% down to 0.1% (100%, 50%, 10%, 1%, 0.5% and 0.1%). For all databases, the two first steps presented re-identification risk = 1 (100%), data loss = 0 and privacy score = 0.1, which means that the data were not sufficiently anonymized and can be easily re-identified. From the third step on, the k-anonymity was applied and, as expected, the re-identification risk decreases while data loss increases (the value of k increases, implying that the dataset anonymity level increases).

There are some steps that, even defining different risk threshold, present the same results (e.g., in Medicine Sales Dataset, the results for 100% and 50% risk threshold). It happens because the k-anonymity needs to provide a value of k whose respective re-identification risk is lower than the acceptable one. In some cases, the value of k satisfies this condition for more than one risk threshold.

The privacy scores were calculated according to the quality model and the highest privacy scores for each dataset are highlighted (the same reason mentioned above is responsible for the identical scores for more than one risk threshold). It is important to observe that, at these highlighted scores, the re-identification risk reached a value lower than the established threshold in the quality model (0.05) and also the data loss is lower than its threshold (0.7). These results give an indication that, to these datasets, the highest privacy score represents the scenario where the thresholds are respected and the best result is obtained considering the trade-off between data privacy and data utility.

Still in Fig. 2, regarding the attacks, *Possibilities* shows the lowest number of possibilities that a unique known record could find a match in the anonymized table. The *# Attacks* is the amount of records that presented the lowest number of possibilities of a match in the anonymized table. So, the higher the *Possibilities*, the lower the re-identification risk. Also, the possibilities can not be lower than the k-value. It means that, for the highest privacy score, the best k-value is applied and guarantees that the possibilities of re-identifying individuals (i.e., de-anonymize the data) is according to this k.

Regarding the overall results in Fig. 3, although the datasets are quite diverse in terms of quantity of records, context and data composition (semi identifiers and data sensitivity), we obtained, for the experiments, similar results for the best score of each dataset.

4   Lessons Learned and Conclusions

This work presented a study on the usefulness of a Quality Model (QM) as a way to characterize a system/service attribute. We presented a quality model instance, i.e., a quality model for privacy, and we analyzed whether the model guides the configuration of the attributes in terms of normalization ranges, thresholds and weights and whether their scores (a quality model result) represent a good characterization of a system considering eight diverse datasets.

We got some interesting observations while calculating privacy scores using the privacy quality model. The first one is that quality models are structures that can be adequate and flexible to represent trustworthiness properties, specially because we could define it for privacy. We believe that, as well as for privacy, it is possible to easily define quality models for other trustworthiness properties, composing them to have a more complete trustworthiness score.

Also, we observed that the privacy quality model allowed to define weights and thresholds for the properties, which provided more flexible configurations and, consequently, a better way to handle the trade-off between anonymization and data utility. This was demonstrated through the experiments, where the highest privacy score was reached when both thresholds (risk and data loss) were respected (see Fig. 2), i.e., those scores represent the best balance between anonymity level and data loss for the dataset.

Regarding the use of PRIVAaaS, it was possible to observe that k-anonymity can deal with thresholds and it is adequate to assure the control over the re-identification risk level that is supposed to be tolerated by the dataset. This was demonstrated through the attacks: when the best k-value (i.e., the k that attends the risk threshold) is applied, the possibilities of re-identifying individuals is according to this k. Furthermore, increasing k is a good solution to be used in the trustworthiness adaptive control loop and improve data privacy protection, contributing to improve the overall trustworthiness of the system.

For future work, other quality models will be created to characterize other trustworthiness properties. Additionally, the scores will be incorporated to the system so it can dispatch adaptations when the score does not meet any expected level.

Acknowledgment. This work has been partially supported by the **ATMOSPHERE** project, funded by Brazilian MCTI/RNP and by the European Commission under the Horizon 2020 grant agreement.

References

1. Basso, T., Matsunaga, R., Moraes, R., Antunes, N.: Challenges on anonymity, privacy, and big data. In: 2016 Seventh Latin-American Symposium on Dependable Computing (LADC), pp. 164–171. IEEE (2016)
2. Dujmovic, J., Elnicki, R.: A DMS cost/benefit decision model: mathematical models for data management system evaluation, comparison, and selection, pp. 82–374. National Bureau of Standards, Washington DC, No. GCR (1982)
3. Friginal, J., Martínez, M., de Andres, D., Ruiz, J.C.: Multi-criteria analysis of measures in benchmarking: dependability benchmarking as a case study. J. Syst. Softw. **111**, 105–118 (2016)
4. Henschke, A., Ford, S.B.: Cybersecurity, trustworthiness and resilient systems: guiding values for policy. J. Cyber Policy **2**(1), 82–95 (2017)
5. ISO/IEC: Software product quality requirements and evaluation - SQUARE. User guide. ISO/IEC (2005)
6. International Organization for Standardization: When the world agrees (ISO/IEC) (2014). https://www.iso.org/standard/64764.html
7. Kort, S., Rudina, E.: The resilience model supporting IIoT system trustworthiness. IIC J. Innov. **1**(1), 1–16 (2018)
8. Kreutz, D., Feitosa, E., Cunha, H., Niedermayer, H., Kinkelin, H.: Increasing the resilience and trustworthiness of openid identity providers for future networks and services. In: 2014 Ninth International Conference on Availability, Reliability and Security, pp. 317–324. IEEE (2014)
9. Medeiros, N.P.D.S., Ivaki, N.R., Da Costa, P.N., Vieira, M.P.A.: Towards an approach for trustworthiness assessment of software as a service. In: 2017 IEEE International Conference on Edge Computing (EDGE), pp. 220–223. IEEE (2017)
10. Mei, H., Huang, G., Xie, T.: Internetware: a software paradigm for internet computing. Computer **45**(6), 26–31 (2012)
11. Sweeney, L.: k-anonymity: a model for protecting privacy. Int. J. Uncertain. Fuzziness Knowl.-Based Syst. **10**(05), 557–570 (2002)

Author Index

Printed in the United States
By Bookmasters